The Islamist Threat
in Southeast Asia:
A Reassessment

Policy Studies 37

The Islamist Threat in Southeast Asia:

A Reassessment

John T. Sidel

The Islamist Threat in Southeast Asia: A Reassessment
by John T. Sidel

East-West Center Washington
1819 L Street, NW, Suite 200
Washington, D.C. 20036
Tel: (202) 293-3995
Fax: (202) 293-1402
E-mail: publications@eastwestcenterwashington.org
Website: www.eastwestcenterwashington.org
Online at: www.eastwestcenterwashington.org/publications

The *Policy Studies* series contributes to the East-West Center's role as a forum for discussion of key contemporary domestic and international political, economic, and strategic issues affecting Asia. The views expressed are those of the author(s) and not necessarily those of the Center.

The publication is supported by a generous grant from the Carnegie Corporation of New York.

First co-published in Singapore in 2007 by ISEAS Publishing
Institute of Southeast Asian Studies
30 Heng Mui Keng Terrace
Pasir Panjang Road
Singapore 119614
E-mail: publish@iseas.edu.sg
Website: <http://bookshop.iseas.edu.sg>

ISEAS Library Cataloguing-in-Publication Data

Sidel, John Thayer, 1966–
    The Islamist threat in Southeast Asia : a reassessment.
    (East-West Center Washington policy studies, 1547-1349 ; PS37)
    1. Islam—Southeast Asia.
    2. Islam—Southeast Asia—History.
    3. Islam and state—Southeast Asia.
    4. Islam and politics—Southeast Asia.
    I. Title
    II. Series: Policy studies (East-West Center Washington) ; 37.
DS1 E13P no. 37   2007

ISBN 978-981-230-489-6 (soft cover)
ISBN 978-981-230-490-2 (PDF)
ISSN 1547-1349 (soft cover)
ISSN 1547-1330 (PDF)

Typeset in Singapore by Superskill Graphics Pte Ltd
Printed in Singapore by Seng Lee Press Pte Ltd

Contents

John T. Sidel

List of Acronyms

ABIM	Angkatan Belia Islam Malaysia (Islamic Youth of Malaysia)
ARMM	Autonomous Region of Muslim Mindanao
BIN	Badan Intelijen Negara (National Intelligence Agency)
CSIS	Center for Strategic and International Studies (Jakarta)
DDII	Dewan Dakwah Islamiyah Indonesia (Islamic Propagation Council of Indonesia)
DPR	Dewan Perwakilan Rakyat (People's Representative Assembly)
FPI	Front Pembela Islam (Front for the Defenders of Islam)
IAIN	Institut Agama Islam Negeri (State Islamic Institute)
ICG	International Crisis Group
ICMI	Ikatan Cendekiawan Muslimin se-Indonesia (All-Indonesian Association of Islamic Intellectuals)
JIL	Jaringan Islam Liberal (Liberal Islam Network)
KOMPAK	Komite Aksi Penanggulangan Akibat Krisis (Crisis Response Action Committee)
MILF	Moro Islamic Liberation Front
MNLF	Moro National Liberation Front
MPR	Majelis Permusyawaratan Rakyat (People's Consultative Assembly)
MUI	Majelis Ulama Indonesia (Council of Indonesian Islamic Scholars)

John T. Sidel

NU	Nahdlatul Ulama
PAN	Partai Amanat Nasional (National Mandate Party)
PAS	Parti Islam se-Malaysia (All-Malaysian Islamic Party)
PBB	Partai Bulan Bintang (Crescent Star Party)
PDI-P	Partai Demokrasi Indonesia—Perjuangan (Indonesian Democratic Party of Struggle)
PKB	Partai Kebangkitan Bangsa (National Awakening Party)
PKI	Partai Komunis Indonesia (Indonesian Communist Party)
PKS	Partai Keadilan Sejahtera (Prosperous Justice Party)
PPP	Partai Persatuan Pembangunan (United Development Party)
SBPAC	Southern Border Provinces Administrative Center
UMNO	United Malays Nationalist Organisation

Executive Summary

In the wake of the September 11 attacks of 2001, Southeast Asia emerged as a major arena in the so-called Global War on Terrorism. Beginning with the Bali bombings of October 2002, Indonesia experienced a series of terrorist attacks apparently perpetrated by a hitherto obscure Islamist group known as Jemaah Islamiyah. Even as suspected members and affiliates of this group were discovered and detained in Malaysia, Singapore, the Philippines, and Thailand, the bombing campaign continued in Indonesia. By 2004, violence in the majority-Muslim provinces of Southern Thailand had reached unprecedented levels, while a new series of detonations attributed to the shadowy Abu Sayyaf Group claimed dozens of lives in the Philippines.

These attacks have combined with a set of apparent social and political trends to offer the picture of a broadly defined Islamist threat in Southeast Asia, embodied not only in terrorist attacks but also in increasing assertiveness and aggression by forces claiming to speak in the name of Islam. Evidence for such putative trends has been found in Indonesia, in the increasing electoral success of the supposedly "fundamentalist" party PKS, in the activities of local Islamic vigilante groups in various cities, and in a range of local experiments with Islamic law by district governments around the archipelago. Meanwhile, in Malaysia, new legislation and legal battles have served to highlight the prominent role of Islam in public life in the country, even as the violence of recent years is presumed to have heightened minority

John T. Sidel

Muslim identity and alienation in the southern provinces of the Philippines and Thailand.

Indeed, the past several years have witnessed a steady stream of academic, think tank, and journalistic coverage of this "Islamist threat" in Southeast Asia. A number of specialists on terrorism have emerged as prolific authors and prominent commentators on this supposed menace to the region. Most notable among them is the American scholar Zachary Abuza, whose writings have exemplified—and amplified—the alarmist picture sketched above. Meanwhile, the episodes of religious violence in Southeast Asia have occasioned a steady stream of reportage on Islamist terrorism in the region, ranging from the fine-grained investigative work pioneered by Sidney Jones of the International Crisis Group to more sensationalistic journalistic coverage. This coverage combined with media reports on a wide range of other Islamist activities provides an overall picture of the region that spotlights Islamist violence, assertiveness, and aggression. Even as many writers offer caveats and qualifications in their depiction of these trends, as yet there has been no serious attempt to offer an overarching alternative account of these developments in the region.

Against this backdrop, this study provides a critical reexamination of the alarmist picture of the region sketched above. In descriptive terms, it argues that the depiction of an ascendant, assertive, aggressive set of Islamist forces in Southeast Asia is not only exaggerated but also fundamentally misleading. Instead of an Islamist offensive, the past several years have witnessed a marked pattern of decline, defeat, disappointment, demobilization, and disentanglement from state power for forces identified with Islamist causes in the region. In both Indonesia and Malaysia, this downward trend followed immediately upon a rising tide of Islamist mobilization in the 1990s, while in the southern provinces of Thailand and the Philippines, local Muslim powerbrokers simultaneously suffered a marked decline in influence, resources, and leverage vis-à-vis non-Muslim politicians in the national arena compared to the patterns of accommodation and cooperation observed in the preceding decade. Overall, today Islamist forces in Southeast Asia are more demobilized, demoralized, disenfranchised, and divided than they have been for many years.

In analytical terms, moreover, the study offers an alternative to the narrowly—and problematically—actor-centered and ideological explanations provided in alarmist accounts of Islamist activities in the region. After all, even the most detailed and well-documented narratives of Islamist terrorist activity in Southeast Asia identify individuals and groups ideologically disposed and logistically trained to engage in violence against alleged enemies of the faith, but fail to explain the specific timing, locations, targets, and forms that such violence has—and has not—assumed. By contrast, a proper contextualization of Islam in Southeast Asia reveals the close correspondence between decline, demobilization, demoralization, and division on the one hand, and the resort to violence and aggression on the other. Thus the explanation offered for the extent, nature, and limits of the Islamist threat across the major Muslim areas of Southeast Asia stresses the aggression of anti-Islamists and non-Muslims on the one hand, and the weakness, insecurity, and fractiousness of the Islamist forces themselves. The explanatory powers of this argument are demonstrated by a comparative analysis of the patterns of Islamist violence and aggression observed across the region in recent years.

As suggested by the title, this monograph offers a reexamination of the nature, position, and trajectory of the forces mobilized behind the banner of Islam in the major Muslim areas of Southeast Asia, namely Indonesia, Malaysia, southern Thailand, and the southern Philippines. This reassessment offers an overarching alternative framework for the description and explanation of patterns of Islamist mobilization, both violent and nonviolent, across Southeast Asia in recent years. In its concluding section, moreover, the monograph also suggests the implications of this reassessment for policy makers and others interested in the future of Southeast Asia.

The Islamist Threat in Southeast Asia: A Reassessment

In the aftermath of the September 11, 2001 attacks on New York City and Washington, D.C., Southeast Asia was quickly identified as a region facing a serious, but hitherto largely ignored or underestimated, Islamist threat (Gershman 2002). In the first instance, this threat was narrowly understood in terms of Islamist terrorist activities. In short order, a series of arrests in Malaysia, the Philippines, and Singapore drew attention to a previously obscure terrorist network identified as Jemaah Islamiyah, accused of close links with Al-Qaeda and said to be based in Indonesia. With the October 2002 bombing of a nightclub in Bali, moreover, the reality of this threat in Indonesia was more firmly established, and it was subsequently confirmed by explosions at the Marriott Hotel in Jakarta in 2003, outside the Australian Embassy in Jakarta in 2004, and again in Bali in late 2005. Meanwhile, a series of bombings in the Philippines attributed to the shadowy Abu Sayyaf Group, and a marked upsurge of violence in the Muslim provinces of southern Thailand, suggested the broader regional nature of the problem. Thus the past several years have witnessed the proliferation of journalistic, academic, think tank, and government reports and studies concerned with the Islamist threat in Southeast Asia, from the well-researched, finely documented, and highly nuanced analysis produced by the widely respected Indonesia specialist Sidney Jones and her collaborators for the International Crisis Group (ICG), to a wide range of more derivative accounts.

Beyond the narrow threat of terrorist activities that this growing body of literature focuses on, moreover, a broader Islamist threat to the polities and societies of Southeast Asia has also been identified. The highly problematic term "Islamist" here refers to the broad range of movements, organizations, and political parties mobilized in avowed defense of Islam as a body of beliefs and a community of believers, and in avowed promotion of the Islamization of state and society. Evidence of this broader threat was first adduced from the emergence and spread of interreligious violence in 1999–2001 in areas of Indonesia such as the Central Sulawesi regency of Poso and the provinces of Maluku and Maluku Utara, and from the mobilization of armed Islamist groups such as Laskar Jihad to assist Muslims in the fighting in these localities. This impression has been sustained and enhanced by the subsequent strong showing of the seemingly "fundamentalist" party PKS (Partai Keadilan Sejahtera or Prosperous Justice Party) in the 2004 parliamentary elections, reports of attacks on churches in West Java in 2005, and media coverage of anti-pornography legislation in Jakarta and local initiatives to implement Islamic law in various regencies around the country in 2006. Meanwhile, ongoing disputes over the role of Islam in public life in Malaysia and continuing violence in southern Thailand and the southern Philippines have helped to present a plausible picture of broader Islamist activity, influence, and assertiveness throughout Muslim areas of Southeast Asia.

Indeed, this purported wider Islamist threat in the region has attracted considerable attention from academics, journalists, and policy makers, as seen in the steady stream of articles, reports, and studies on related topics over the past several years. This trend is perhaps best exemplified by Zachary Abuza, an American academic, prolific author, and frequent media commentator whose work has come to enjoy broad circulation and coverage. Over the past several years, Abuza has produced a series of books, reports, and articles presenting a distinctly alarmist picture of Islam in Southeast Asia, beginning with a 2003 account of Al-Qaeda's infiltration of Southeast Asia and continuing with a series of journal articles, working papers, and Internet postings that depict the

> *[the] Islamist threat [in Southeast Asia]...has attracted considerable attention*

region in terms of continuing or growing Islamist terrorist activities in Indonesia, the southern Philippines, and southern Thailand (Abuza 2003, 2004, 2005, 2006). In a recently published book on Indonesia, moreover, Abuza links the terrorist activities of these "hard-core" activists to a broader set of Islamist forces in Indonesia today, who are described by Abuza as providing a sympathetic audience of "fellow travellers," a mass base, and a source of recruitment for terrorist activities as well as other forms of violence against non-Muslims and Muslims deemed insufficiently pious or puritanical (Abuza 2007). In short, Abuza provides an influential overview of trends in Southeast Asia that suggests the continuing, if not growing, seriousness of a broadly construed Islamist threat in the region.

This monograph questions the nature and extent of this Islamist threat and offers something of a corrective to the rather alarmist picture it paints. As suggested in the pages below, there are many reasons to question the descriptive accuracy and explanatory power of the alarmist picture of an insurgent, aggressive, and cohesive Islamist movement in Southeast Asia. Indeed, the vast majority of serious writings on Islam in the region, whether journalistic or scholarly, are careful to note the limitations, contradictions, and internal tensions of this Islamist threat, even as the cumulative effect of all the attention supports an underlying sense of continuing menace. Yet overall, caveats and qualifications notwithstanding, the spotlighting of Islamist terrorist activities, of other isolated incidents of Islamist aggression, and of pockets of Islamist influence works to exaggerate the Islamist threat and to obscure major trends working against Islamist forces in Southeast Asia.

A more balanced, nuanced, and properly contextualized analysis of Islamist terrorist activities and broader Islamist influence and assertiveness in the region as a whole is needed to understand recent trends and developments, and to appreciate their implications for Southeast Asia in the years to come. Drawing on the rich body of scholarly literature on Islam in Southeast Asia, a wide range of media sources, and the author's own research in Indonesia and the Philippines, this monograph offers a broad overview of trends in Southeast Asia that suggests an understanding of the Islamist threat in the region that is very different from the accounts written in an alarmist vein. In contrast with alarmist depictions of a growing Islamist threat in Southeast Asia, the pages below outline a pattern of demobilization, dissension, disappointment, and disentanglement from state power for major Islamist forces in Indonesia and Malaysia in recent years, along with parallel declines and defeats for those championing the causes of Muslim separatism in the southern provinces of the Philippines and Thailand. Against the narrowly—and problematically—actor-centered and ideological accounts of Islamist terrorist violence, moreover, this study offers a properly contextualized explanation for the specific timing, locations, perpetrators, targets, and forms of such violence in terms of both internal and external threats to the structures of religious authority and identity associated with Islam. Thus, unlike the identification of incidents of Islamist terrorist violence with aggression and assertiveness by a broader range of Islamist forces, the argument posed here traces a very different kind of causal relationship between them. Overall, this monograph provides the basis for a fully elaborated descriptive and explanatory framework that is an alternative to the alarmist accounts associated with Abuza and others.

Weaknesses of the Alarmist Account

There are at least two reasons to question the descriptive, evidentiary basis for the prevailing alarmist picture of the Islamist terrorist threat in Southeast Asia. First, this picture is based on an uncritical overreliance on official sources drawn from the security services of the region. This tendency is most pronounced in the work of "terrorism experts" such as Abuza who have little expertise in the countries of the region. Even some of the well-documented ICG reports, however, cite sworn statements of jailed terrorist suspects without questioning the interrogation conditions under which they were produced (intimidation, extortion, and torture of prisoners are routine practices).[1]

> *the prevailing alarmist picture...is based on an uncritical overreliance on official sources*

Neither excessive cynicism nor elaborate conspiracy theorizing is necessary to raise doubts about the credibility of various Southeast Asian security services as definitive sources of information. All of the governments in the region, after all, have a strong interest in establishing themselves as firm allies of the United States in the so-called Global War on Terrorism, with their security services in particular clearly standing to benefit in budgetary and other ways from well-publicized participation in this struggle. The Indonesian, Malaysian, Philippine, Singaporean, and Thai governments have also been pursuing domestic agendas for which the pursuit of Islamist terrorist cells provides useful "cover," as discussed below. It would be naïve or disingenuous, then, to assume that the security services' selective provision of access and information to researchers is not colored by these broader interests and agendas. Even the white paper published by Singapore's Ministry of Home Affairs raises eyebrows with its repeated references to supposed Jemaah Islamiyah terrorist plans that proceeded only to the reconnaissance stage and were "eventually not pursued, for unknown reasons" (Singapore Ministry of Home Affairs 2003: 9, 13, 29). Indeed, the white paper concludes with the frank admission that "none of these plans against Singapore targets had proceeded beyond reconnaissance to the more serious stages of preparations (e.g. procurement of explosives)" (Ibid.: 31).

More generally, the security services of most of these countries have a long history of duplicity and double-dealing, as seen both in a broad range of corrupt activities and human rights abuses in general, and in their interaction with Islamist groups in particular. In the Philippines, for example, knowledgeable observers have long cited evidence of police and military collusion or even coordination with the Abu Sayyaf Group in its kidnapping and extortion activities. The history of informal accommodations between armed Muslim separatist groups such as the Moro Islamic Liberation Front (MILF) and elements in the government is also well known (Torres 2001: 145–48; Burnham 2003: 149–50; Gutierrez and Borras 2004: 23–27). In Indonesia, moreover, there is a long history of military intelligence infiltration and manipulation of Islamist groups, dating back at least to the 1970s (Jenkins 1984: 53–56; Cahyono 1992: 70–93; 1998: 70–73, 92–94, 182–84; Conboy 2004: 140–42). The wave of terrorist bombings in Indonesia in recent years coincided with the tenure of (Ret.) Lt. Gen. A. M. Hendropriyono as head of the National Intelligence Agency (Badan Intelijen Negara or BIN), a tenure that ended ignominiously with accusations of BIN involvement in several murders, narcotics trafficking, and currency counterfeiting (*Tempo* 2005a: 26–29; 2005b: 30–31).

Hendropriyono had a long history of links with the very same network of Islamist militants accused of responsibility for the bombings of 2002–05 in Indonesia. This network stemmed from an Islamic boarding school, Pesantren Al-Mukmin, in Ngruki, Sukoharjo, whose founders were arrested and imprisoned in the late 1970s and forced into exile in the mid-1980s for their Islamist views. The caretakers of the *pesantren* were forced to allow the security services and its agents access to the school and an active role in its management (Assegaff 1995: 50–51). In 1989, Hendropriyono, then serving as an army colonel, had led troops in the massacre of members of an Islamic intentional community founded by a group of fugitive Ngruki graduates in a remote village in the Sumatran province of Lampung (Al Chaidar 2000; Syukur 2003). In subsequent years, as Hendropriyono rose to positions of considerable prominence and power in Jakarta, he assiduously attempted to achieve some kind of reconciliation with the survivors of this massacre. During his stint as minister for transmigration, he provided them with financial assistance, employment in his various businesses, placement in government posts, and even land for resettlement (Awwas 2000). Thus when Hendropriyono assumed the directorship of BIN in late 2001, he had already cultivated a coterie of clients and informants from within the network of Ngruki alumni. It was against this backdrop that police investigators, journalists, and other researchers discovered numerous links (e.g., cell phone conversations) between Indonesian army and intelligence officers and some of the activists arrested and charged with terrorist bombings (*Tempo* 2001b: 68; 2001c: 71–72; 2001d: 76; 2001e: 78–79; 2001f: 80; 2002a). In short, there is ample reason to treat official accounts of Islamist terrorism in Southeast Asia with at least a small measure of skepticism, and to subject the security services of the region to more critical scrutiny.

A second reason to question the prevailing alarmist picture of the Islamist terrorist threat in Southeast Asia is that it leaves entirely unanswered crucial questions about the nature and extent of these activities. For even if the security services are treated as unimpeachable sources of information about the terrorist activities that have occurred in Southeast Asia in recent years, neither these sources nor the literature that draws on them can account for the timing, locations, targets, and outcomes of terrorist violence in the region. These sources, and the authors who draw on them, concur in their identification of specific terrorist groups such as Jemaah Islamiyah and Abu Sayyaf as responsible for bombings in various parts of Southeast Asia. What remains unexplained, however, is the timing of these groups' attacks, the choice of locations—foreign, Western targets in Indonesia but local ones in Thailand and the Philippines—and the outcomes of these attacks beyond the number of fatalities caused. Why, after all, has Islamist violence in Indonesia, the most populous Muslim country in the world, been seemingly reduced to a single annual bomb explosion over the past few years? Why have terrorist attacks in the Philippines been restricted to Filipino targets? Why has violence in Thailand been restricted to the southern Muslim provinces of the country? Not simply what little violence *has* occurred, but also how much violence has *not*, cries out for explanation.

> *how much violence has not [occurred], cries out for explanation*

Such doubts as to the descriptive accuracy and explanatory power of the prevailing picture of Islamist terrorism are also applicable to the broader realm of Islamist influence, activity, and assertiveness in Southeast Asia. The sources of information on this broader Islamist threat, after all, are overwhelmingly anti-Islamist in orientation and opposed to the extension of Islamist influence in the social and political life of the region, while many of the Islamist sources cited are also misleadingly triumphalist in tone, trumpeting successes that are exaggerated or unrepresentative of broader trends.

In Muslim-majority Indonesia, for example, there is a tendency to depict the small Christian minority as vulnerable victims, and to highlight the abuses and injustices inflicted by Islamist forces on Muslims and non-Muslims alike. Yet in fact, the well-publicized "anti-Chinese riots" of 1995–98 left hundreds more Muslim than ethnic-Chinese casualties in their wake. In the violence waged by armed Christian and Muslim groups in Central Sulawesi, Maluku, and Maluku Utara in 1999–2001, moreover, Muslims were amply represented among those killed, and armed Christian groups were responsible for some of the worst incidents of collective violence. Such large-scale interreligious conflict was also confined to a relatively small area of Indonesia and lasted roughly three years before stalemate, exhaustion, and de-escalation set in, and there has been virtually no resumption of large-scale collective violence in these localities since the end of 2001 (Sidel 2006: 68–195). Similarly, when American journalists bewail the oppressiveness of life under the *shari'a* code in the Islamic state of Malaysia or in the Islamist-run localities in Indonesia, they do so without reference to common problems of exploitation and abuse of human rights fostered by secular legal conditions in these countries. In short, coverage of Southeast Asia can be both selective and sensationalist with regard to Islamist trends.

Overall, this problem of what social scientists call "selection bias" makes for a distorted picture of the nature and direction of trends in Islamist influence, activity, and assertiveness in Southeast Asia. For whatever the current strengths of Islamist movements in Southeast Asia today, they clearly represent a marked reduction from those experienced at the turn of the twenty-first century just seven years ago. This is apparent if one considers trends over the past seven years in the four major Muslim areas of Southeast Asia—Indonesia, Malaysia, the southern Philippines, and southern Thailand—as described below.

Beyond these doubts about the descriptive accuracy of the alarmist literature, its selection bias also makes for very limited explanatory power. Just as Islamist terrorists are understood to launch terrorist attacks, except when and where they do not, so are broader Islamist forces seen to be active, assertive, and influential, except when and where they are not. There is nothing like a framework of analysis that allows for an understanding of patterns of change and variation in Islamist terrorist activities or in Islamist forces and fortunes more broadly. A clearer, more coherent, and more compelling account is needed, one that goes beyond a description of the various forms of mobilization—violent and nonviolent, successful and unsuccessful—undertaken in the name of Islam in Southeast Asia in recent years, and offers something closer to an explanation for the overall patterns observed.

An Alternative Approach

The remainder of this monograph offers an alternative approach to the prevailing picture of the Islamist threat in Southeast Asia sketched above. This approach is adopted from a broad body of established scholarly literature on terrorism and Islamist activity in other parts of the world, and applied to Southeast Asian conditions. The resulting account covers both the narrow realm of Islamist terrorist activity in Southeast Asia and the broader realm of Islamist influence in Muslim areas of the region. Indeed, beyond a revisionist description of the Islamist threat in Southeast Asia, an explanation is offered for recent trends, one that links Islamist terrorist activities systematically to broader shifts in Islamist influence over time.

This approach follows the conclusions drawn by the sociologist Michele Wieviorka in his research on the use of terrorist violence by Basque and Palestinian nationalists and German and Italian left-wing radicals. "The organized practice of indiscriminate and irredeemable violence," Wieviorka argues, "is not a faltering movement's last best hope or final act of desperation but rather a substitute for a movement which has either become imaginary or has fallen out of sync with the hopes pinned on it" (Wieviorka 2004: 291). He concludes,

> In its purest—and most extreme—manifestations, terrorism always betrays the disintegration of some collective action. Wherever the social, national, or communal consciousness is strong, and wherever a social or any other kind of movement is capable of being formed, there can be no place for terrorist spinoffs. These appear, and take shape—and become rationales of action rather than mere situational combat strategies—through the disintegration of a collective consciousness, or in the collapse, breakdown, or failure of a social, national, or communist movement. (Ibid.: 297)

A similar argument has been applied by Olivier Roy, the prominent French specialist on Islamist movements, to the rise of transnational *jihadist* networks like Al-Qaeda at the turn of the twenty-first century. The rise of Al-Qaeda, Roy argues, came as a response to the co-optation, defeat, or disintegration of various Islamist movements in the 1990s and, more broadly, the "deterritorialization" of Islam and the consequent weakening of this religion's social authority (Roy 1995, 2004; Kepel 2000). "Radical militant jihadists," Roy notes, "fight at the frontier [of the Muslim world] to protect a centre where they have no place. They fight not to protect a territory but to re-create a community. They are besieged in a fortress they do not inhabit" (Roy 2004: 289).

Overall, this tradition of scholarship on both terrorist activities and Islamist movements suggests a very different descriptive and explanatory approach for understanding the Islamist threat in Southeast Asia from the prevailing one. Recent Islamic terrorism in the region, in this alternative view, is best understood as a phenomenon intimately bound up with the political, sociological, and discursive trends of the past several years, trends that have worked to undermine the possibilities for articulating claims and mobilizing people under the sign of Islam. Terrorist violence in Southeast Asia, in other words, reflects not the strength and solidity of insurgent Islamist forces in the region, but rather their weakness, their fragmentation, and the threat of their dissolution.

> *Terrorist violence...reflects [the weakness]...of insurgent Islamist forces*

Yet even here, a continuing focus on the Islamists alone may obscure—and thus excuse—the active role of their enemies, both national and international, in spurring the shift to terrorist violence and the globalization of their *jihad*.[2] As Muhammed Hafez has argued in his study of Islamist violence throughout the Muslim world:

> Muslims become violently militant when they encounter exclusionary states that deny them meaningful access to political institutions and employ indiscriminate repressive policies against their citizens during periods of mass mobilization. Political exclusion and state repression unleash a dynamic of radicalization characterized by exclusive rebel organizations that isolate Islamists from their broader society and foster anti-system ideologies that frame the potentially healthy competition between secularism and Islamism as a mortal struggle between faith and impiety. The cumulative effect of political repression, exclusive organizations, and anti-system ideologies is protracted conflicts against secular ruling regimes and ordinary civilians who are perceived as sustaining those regimes. (Hafez 2003: xv–xvi)

Indeed, alongside—in fact, overshadowing—the transnational networks of Islamic scholars and pilgrims, Islamist activists, and Al-Qaeda operatives linking Southeast Asia to other parts of the Muslim world are the thicker webs of power and influence connecting the security services and other agencies of Southeast Asian governments to centers of power in Washington, D.C., London, Tokyo, and Canberra. Accompanying the attractive "pull" of global *jihad* for Southeast Asian Islamists disappointed and demoralized by reversals and declines in their local struggles—and drawn to the possibilities opened up by Osama bin Laden and Al-Qaeda—has been the aggressive "push" by anti-Islamist forces in Southeast Asia encouraged by the United States and its allies (most notably Australia). The year 2001, after all, witnessed not only the September 11 attacks on New York City and Washington, D.C., but also the inauguration of new governments in Jakarta, Manila, and Bangkok with especially weak links—and strong antipathies—to Islamist movements in their respective countries, discernible tendencies to rely on national military institutions to consolidate power, and urgent imperatives to strengthen ties with the new Republican administration of George W. Bush in the United States. As argued below, a contextual analysis of the national and international dimensions of this broader conjuncture in Southeast Asian politics provides an illuminating prism through which to understand the specific patterns of terrorist violence and Islamist mobilization observed in the region over the past several years. But first some historical background is necessary to allow for the kind of perspective required for rigorous comparative analysis of the patterns observed.

Historical Backdrop: Western Colonialism and the Subjugation of Islam in Southeast Asia

In order to appreciate the broader context of Islamist activities and influence in Southeast Asia, and the antagonism between Islamist forces and those identified with the West in the region, it is essential to understand the ways in which European and American colonial rule created lasting obstacles to the promotion of Islamist politics in Southeast Asia. The intrusions of the Portuguese, Spanish, Dutch, British, French, and American empires in Southeast Asia, after all, not only introduced Christianity to the region, but also divided Muslims through the erection of state borders and other barriers that divided them administratively. Over time, these intrusions also reinforced existing linguistic and cultural differences among them. More importantly, perhaps, the incorporation of Southeast Asia into the world capitalist economy under conditions of colonial rule established the enduring subordination of Muslims to non-Muslims in the market, even as the construction of modern colonial states in the region established enduring patterns of subordination of Islamic traditions of learning and socialization (and thus of acquiring cultural and social capital) to those pioneered in the Christian West and reconfigured as "secular." These legacies prefigured the notably profane—indeed, at times obscene—forms of machine politics, money politics, and oligarchic rule so prevalent today throughout much of Southeast Asia. No account of the Islamist threat in Southeast Asia is

John T. Sidel

complete without a full acknowledgment of the nature and extent of these legacies and a deep understanding of the origins and aims of struggles in the name of Islam in the region.

These legacies are evident if we consider the Indonesian archipelago, where the spread of Islam had proceeded for a few hundred years before the arrival of the Dutch East India Company in the seventeenth century, but where the gradual consolidation of Dutch colonial rule constrained the promotion of the Muslim faith in at least three decisive ways. First of all, the gradual creation of a modern state was achieved through the incorporation, subordination, and bureaucratization of local aristocracies in Java and elsewhere in archipelago, with the various sultanates of what became the Netherlands East Indies increasingly stripped of authority over religious affairs and encouraged instead to develop local culture—and codify local custom (*adat*)—in ways that reinforced parochial particularisms and reified ethnic divisions among Muslims (Pemberton 1994). As Dutch rule spread and deepened in the late nineteenth and twentieth centuries, moreover, these local aristocrats were retooled into bureaucrats whose entry into and ascendancy within the rapidly expanding colonial state spurred the creation of a modern secular school system, out of which many leaders of the Indonesian nationalist movement would eventually emerge. For both the Dutch colonial regime and the Indonesian nationalist movement in the early twentieth century, modern secular education thus came to supplement, if not fully supplant, the set of aristocratic lineages and traditions rigidified and reinvented under the Dutch as the basis for claims to rule over the archipelago. Thus the political class that emerged out of the nationalist movement was one in which graduates of Islamic schools represented a disadvantaged minority, and in which understandings of Islam were colored—and, according to some, compromised—by ethnic, cultural, customary, and theological diversity (Kahin 1952; Anderson 1972).

Second, under Dutch colonial auspices the spread and deepening of capitalist market relations in the Indonesian archipelago were pioneered by a comprador business class of decidedly non-Muslim complexion. Thanks to Dutch policies of segregation, the small minority of immigrants from southern China and their offspring were sharply defined as "Chinese" and confined to urban ghettos, with assimilation into local societies (especially on Java) and conversion to Islam strongly discouraged. Spurred on by the establishment of the Cultivation System on Java in the mid-nineteenth century, Chinese revenue farmers and merchants expanded their commercial and credit networks deep into the rural hinterlands, firmly establishing themselves as the compradors of the Dutch "plural society" (Rush 1990). With the abandonment of segregation and the abolition of the revenue farms in the early twentieth century, subsequent generations of immigrants from China and their offspring developed into an Indonesia-wide Chinese business class. Thus the world's most populous Muslim country was destined to become one with a decidedly non-Muslim capitalist class. The three decades of rapid economic growth and industrialization under Suharto (1966–98) saw the emergence of a number of well-connected "indigenous" (*pribumi*) businessmen, but the overwhelmingly predominant element in Indonesian business remained—as it does today—Chinese and non-Muslim (Robison and Hadiz 2004).

Third and finally, the Dutch colonial era saw the emergence of a privileged Christian minority within the ranks of the urban professional classes and the expanding colonial state. In various locations around the archipelago, residual Catholic influences from the early Portuguese era (especially in the eastern islands) and Protestant missionary efforts under Dutch (or occasionally English or German) auspices created pockets of Christian identity centered on missionary schools of various denominations and affiliations. Such schools not only introduced these converts to the Bible and to a distinctly modern notion of (Great Tradition) religious faith and identity, but they also served as sites for the recruitment of colonial civil servants, soldiers, teachers, and professionals. This small but privileged minority of Indonesian Christians was destined to be markedly overrepresented in the ranks of the bureaucracy, the army, the universities, and the urban middle class (Jones 1976).

Thus a close connection between Christianity, education, and access to state power was established in the Netherlands East Indies, a relationship that would last well into the era of Indonesian independence. Indeed, Christian prominence in Indonesian public life was so pronounced throughout much of the Suharto era that as late as the mid-1980s, all of the key economic and security portfolios in the cabinet were in Catholic or Protestant hands, the leading Jakarta newspapers were Christian-owned, and the intellectual life of the capital was heavily colored by Jesuit-trained scholars and the Catholic-run think tank CSIS (Center for Strategic and International Studies). Through their positions at Indonesia's top universities, in the military establishment, and CSIS, Christians thus landed themselves and their protégés in the seats of civilian and military power, in the cabinet, in Golkar (the regime's electoral machine), in the regime's pseudo-parliamentary bodies, and in key media outlets and other business ventures (Tanter 1991: 321–25, 420–32). It is no wonder that the Suharto regime was so easily caricatured by Islamists as a government run by Muslim patsies manipulated by a Christian conspiracy to control Indonesia.

Meanwhile, British colonial rule in Malaya from the late nineteenth century left similar but different legacies in independent Malaysia. As the Dutch did in the Netherlands East Indies, the British in Malaya relied on immigrant Chinese merchants as a comprador class, establishing ethnic-Chinese hegemony in the business world that has survived independence and by now more than three decades of affirmative action for "indigenous" (*bumiputra*) capital in Malaysia (Jesudason 1990; Gomez 1999; Searle 1999). The British, however, unlike the Dutch, also relied on immigrant Chinese—and to a lesser extent Indian—labor to fill the ranks of the working classes of the colony, thus swelling the Malay Peninsula with rising numbers of Chinese tin miners and Indian rubber plantation workers, even as the Malay peasantry was essentially encouraged to remain in subsistence agriculture. This massive labor importation guaranteed that Malaysia would have a huge non-Malay and—given British "plural society" policies of segregation—non-Muslim population, in stark contrast with neighboring Indonesia (Freedman 1960; Hirschman 1986). Finally, unlike the Dutch in the Indies, the British firmly subordinated the realm of Islamic education, jurisprudence, and worship to the local aristocracies of the Malay states. As the eminent historian William Roff has noted, "A direct effect of colonial rule was thus to encourage the concentration of doctrinal and administrative religious authority in the hands of a hierarchy of officials directly dependent on the sultans for their position and power" (Roff 1967: 72).

In short, British colonial rule guaranteed that the demographic and electoral position of Muslims in Malaysia would be constrained by the large population of non-Muslims of Chinese and Indian ancestry, that the economic and social position of Muslims would be colored by non-Muslim predominance in the marketplace, and that Islam as a realm of religious worship, education, and association would remain closely controlled by the state. These legacies further guaranteed that the post-independence Malaysian state, however officially "Islamic" its character, would in no small measure be controlled by the secularly educated heirs to the Malay aristocratic elite retooled and reschooled by the British, and by the Chinese business class. Thus, scholars have argued, the administration of Islam in Malaysia has been strongly shaped by state leaders'—not especially Islamic—imperatives of maintaining social control and promoting modernization among the Muslim Malay population (Peletz 2002; Nasr 2001).

Such historically determined constraints on Muslim populations and Islamic possibilities in Indonesia and Malaysia were, of course, paralleled and exceeded by the legacies left by colonial rule on the minority Muslim areas of southern Thailand and the southern Philippines. In the case of southern Thailand, for example, the British imposition of the Bowring Treaty of 1855 set in motion a process of absolutist state centralization, bureaucratization, and internal colonization that, by the turn of the twentieth century, had begun to subordinate previously loosely ruled or tribute-paying principalities—such as the largely Malay-speaking and Muslim sultanate of Patani—to the Ministry of the Interior in Bangkok (Winichakul 1994). With all areas of this newly unified Siam now subordinated to provincial governors and district officers appointed and transferred by Bangkok, and with the growing bureaucracy educated in Thai-language secular schools, local methods of accumulating prestige, power, and knowledge in what became the Muslim south were increasingly marginalized, a pattern that continued after the fall of the Chakri dynasty in 1932, the transformation of Siam into "Thailand," and the consolidation of military rule (McVey 1989). Parallel to this political subordination of the southern provinces to Bangkok was their relegation to the role of peripheral hinterland to the central hub of the emerging national market, through the rice trade, the banking industry, and, in due course, the diversifying agribusiness, commercial, and industrial conglomerates of Sino-Thai businessmen and their foreign partners, all operating out of the national capital (Suehiro 1992). Thus in political, economic, and social terms, Muslims in southern Thailand were firmly subordinated to Bangkok, first under the Chakri monarchy, then under military rule, and finally, with gradual democratization since the 1970s, to a parliament dominated by Sino-Thai businessmen and bankers.

Meanwhile, Spanish and American colonial rule left similar but different legacies for the Muslim population in the southern Philippines. From its inception in the mid-sixteenth century, Spanish colonial rule in the

Philippines was animated by a post-Reconquista zeal to stem the ongoing spread of Islam in the archipelago. Colonization meant evangelization, with lowland areas throughout Luzon, the Visayas, and northern Mindanao effectively Christianized, even as Muslims living under the remaining sultanates of central Mindanao and the Sulu Archipelago were demonized and dubbed "Moros" (Ileto 1971; Scott 1991; Warren 1985). While these Islamicized areas remained uncolonized throughout the duration of the Spanish colonial era, they were eventually "pacified" and officially incorporated under American rule in the first decades of the twentieth century. As elsewhere in the Philippine archipelago, the process of national integration was achieved through elections, first for municipal mayors, then for provincial governors, and in due course for congressmen, senators, and presidents.

Yet for all the promise of this "colonial democracy," Muslim Filipinos remained almost as marginalized as their Thai counterparts and almost equally subordinated to non-Muslim economic and political power. As Muslim areas of Mindanao and the Sulu Archipelago had remained outside the orbit of Spanish colonial rule, they had only belatedly experienced the processes by which the elimination of barriers to free trade in the nineteenth century gave rise to a Chinese *mestizo* comprador class for foreign firms in the prosperous port cities elsewhere in the Philippines. Thus with the incorporation of previously un-Hispanicized, un-Christianized areas into the Philippines in the early twentieth century, the path of internal colonization of Muslim Mindanao and the Sulu Archipelago was opened wide to coconut, corn, and rice millers; moneylenders and bankers; bus, electricity, and shipping companies; and colleges and universities based in Cagayan de Oro, Cebu, Davao, and Manila. This process was facilitated by special arrangements for the "Moro Province" that subordinated local officials to Manila's appointees well into the 1950s. Without locally elected congressmen, and with city mayors and provincial governors appointed by Manila, the dispensation of patronage in Muslim Mindanao and the Sulu Archipelago in the first half of the twentieth century did not allow local Muslim politicians to accumulate as much wealth and power as did their Christian counterparts elsewhere in the archipelago. Logging concessions, pasture lease agreements, transportation franchises, and titles for large tracts of "public" land fell into the hands of carpetbaggers and their allies from Christian areas of Mindanao, Cebu, Iloilo, and Manila (Abinales 2000). Thus, as in southern Thailand, Muslims in the southern Philippines came to be systematically disadvantaged and subordinated vis-à-vis non-Muslims.

Against these kinds of externally imposed constraints on Muslims and on the authority enjoyed by the institutions of the Muslim faith in Southeast Asia, what kind of response has been mounted that today might be identified as the origins of the so-called Islamist threat? In Southeast Asia, as in other

> *Southeast Asia...saw the emergence...of new forms of Islamic consciousness, association, and mobilization*

parts of the Muslim world, the late nineteenth and early twentieth centuries saw the emergence and expansion of new forms of Islamic consciousness, association, and mobilization, trends not only promoted by the incursions of colonial states and the capitalist market, but also encouraged by the late Ottoman sultan Abdulhamid II and greatly enabled by the revolutions in transportation (e.g., railroads, steamships) and communications technology (e.g., newspapers) of the era (Laffan 2002: 114–41; Roff 1967: 32–90; Karpat 2001). In Southeast Asia, as in other parts of the Muslim world, moreover, the last three decades of the twentieth century saw an efflorescence of new Islamist activity, a trend similarly impelled by the establishment of new nation-states and the onset of rapid industrialization and urbanization, aided by generous funding from Saudi Arabia and enormously enhanced by Muslims' expanding literacy and access to radio, television, and, in due course, the Internet. These developments increasingly made it possible for Muslims in Southeast Asia—as elsewhere—to understand their faith as "a coherent system of practices and beliefs, rather than merely an unexamined and unexaminable way of life," to think of "knowing Islam" as "a defined set of beliefs *such as those set down in textbook presentations*," and to put Islam "consciously to work for various types of social and political projects" (Starrett 1998: 9–10).

Yet as suggested by the variegated picture sketched above, the ways in which Muslims have "objectified" and "functionalized" Islam in Southeast Asia have varied across the region, giving rise to different forms of struggles waged under the banner of Islam. In Indonesia, for example, the essential mode of promoting Islam has been education, with modernist Muslims establishing schools, universities, and educational associations to rival the secular and Christian institutions—and the aristocratic and Christian schoolboy networks—that provided such a head start on gaining access to state power in the country. This strategy was evident in the founding in the first two decades of the twentieth century of such modernist educational associations as Muhammadiyah, Persatuan Islam, and Al-Irsyad, and in subsequent efforts to expand these associations' school systems into full-fledged universities and to increase their influence through Islamic university student organizations, media outlets, and political parties.

the ways in which Muslims have "objectified" and "functionalized" Islam...have varied

Meanwhile in Malaysia, the Islamist project has been aimed at the enhancement and elaboration of existing tools of an ostensibly already Islamic state to promote what are said to be more genuinely Islamic goals than those pursued by the ruling Malay elite and its non-Malay partners. On the one hand, this state-centered project has been pursued most assiduously through the capture of state governments by the Islamic party PAS (Parti Islam se-Malaysia) and state-level legislation of new Islamic laws. On the other hand, the ruling party UMNO (United Malays Nationalist Organisation) has incorporated former activists of the Islamic youth group ABIM (Angkatan Belia Islam Malaysia) and used federal state resources and regulatory powers to promote more thoroughgoing Islamization. In southern Thailand and the southern Philippines, by contrast, where Muslims remain overwhelmingly rural, poor, and with limited access to secular or religious education, the struggle for Islam has assumed the form of armed separatist mobilization, with demands for independent states for the Muslim populations in these two marginalized areas.

Thus to paraphrase an old German philosopher, Islamists have made their own history, but they have not made it as they please. They have not made it under self-selected circumstances, but under circumstances transmitted from the past. Muslims have been latecomers and junior partners vis-à-vis non-Muslims in the capitalist market, and avowed representatives of the Islamic faith have been subordinated to secularized Muslim and non-Muslim politicians in the control of state power and policy. Thus the Islamist threat in Southeast Asia has been a counterhegemonic one championed by a disadvantaged minority against the entrenched order of non-Islamic—and, in large measure, non-Muslim—power, wealth, and influence. To understand how Islamist forces in Southeast Asia have in recent years mobilized and mounted various kinds of challenges to this status quo, a closer examination of the contemporary context is in order, first in Muslim-majority Indonesia, and then in Malaysia, southern Thailand, and the southern Philippines.

Indonesia: The Extrusion and Globalization of *Jihad*

Of all the countries in Southeast Asia, Indonesia stands out as the most prominent site for Islamist terrorist activity and broader Islamist influence. It is in Indonesia, after all, where the most frequent and most fatal bombings have occurred in recent years, and Jemaah Islamiyah, the organization identified as the hub of Al-Qaeda-linked or Al-Qaeda-inspired Islamist terrorist activity throughout Southeast Asia, is said to be based in Indonesia and largely led by Indonesians. The terrorist bombings in Indonesia attributed to Jemaah Islamiyah, moreover, have since 2002 targeted sites of foreign influence and power in the country—the Bali nightclubs (October 2002), the Marriott Hotel in Jakarta (August 2003), the Australian Embassy (September 2004), and restaurants catering to tourists on Bali (October 2005)—thus attracting unparalleled international attention. Meanwhile, Indonesia is where Islamist paramilitary groups have intervened in interreligious violence, where Islamist vigilante groups have engaged in intimidation and aggression, where Islamist parties have exerted influence over successive national governments, and where ostensible elements of Islamic law have been selectively imposed in various localities under Islamist control. As during the Cold War and the heyday of Soekarno, the Indonesian Communist Party (Partai Komunis Indonesia or PKI), and the "Communist menace," today Indonesia is regarded as the center of the Islamist threat in the region.

Most accounts portray the bombings of recent years as the work of Jemaah Islamiyah, whose origins, orientation, and activities are described at some length and with varying inflections. At first glance, the identification of the perpetrators as members of Jemaah Islamiyah would appear to suffice as an explanation for the violence of 2000–05. After all, the bombers of Jemaah Islamiyah were distinguished by at least some clandestine links to

Al-Qaeda and Osama bin Laden, by lineages stretching back to the armed Darul Islam movement of the 1950s and early 1960s, and, more broadly, by a loose affiliation and shared orientation with legal, above-ground Islamist organizations in Indonesia—Al-Irsyad, Persatuan Islam, and Dewan Dakwah Islamiyah Indonesia (DDII)—known for their strict puritanism, strident anti-Christian, anti-secular, and anti-Semitic rhetoric, and strong transnational connections to Salafi and Wahhabi currents in Saudi Arabia and Pakistan (Van Bruinessen 2003). This backdrop is amply described in the various reports written by Sidney Jones and published by the International Crisis Group (ICG) over the past few years (International Crisis Group 2002a, 2002b, 2003, 2004a, 2004d, 2005a, 2005c, 2006a).

Yet what remains unexplained is the timing of these bombings, and the shift in the targets of the explosions, from local Christian churches around the archipelago in 2000–2001 to foreign sites in 2002–05. The Persatuan Islam journal *Pembela Islam* (Defender of Islam) was already bemoaning the weakness of Muslims in the face of a dynamic Christianity in the 1930s, and Dewan Dakwah activists were railing against *Kristenisasi* (Christianization) and the closet secularism of liberal, Western-educated and -influenced Muslim intellectuals throughout the 1990s. At no point during these years, however, did any of the thousands of students and graduates of Al-Irsyad and Persatuan Islam schools in Indonesia take up arms or explosive materials, and indeed only a very small fraction did so in the peak years of *jihad* in 2000–05 (International Crisis Group 2004d). Even the attribution—and reduction—of this *jihad* to Al-Qaeda and its operatives leaves crucial questions unanswered: Why was there no paramilitary mobilization or bombing campaign *before* 2000? Why the shift from Indonesian targets to foreign, Western ones in 2002–05? And finally, why was there not more religious violence in Indonesia, but instead its apparent reduction to a single annual explosion by 2005?

As suggested above, the answers to these questions lie in no small measure in the discursive, political, and sociological context of Indonesia at the turn of the twenty-first century, and in the shifting position of Islam within this context. Indeed, the backdrop to the bombings of these years was distinguished by a new configuration of religious authority and power in the country. In contrast with the preceding decade of steady ascendancy and rising assertiveness by forces associated with the promotion of Islam in the Indonesian state and the public sphere, the turn of the century saw the rise and decline of the Islamist project in the country, in a rather sudden and dramatic reversal of fortunes.

Under the auspices of the authoritarian Suharto regime, the 1990s had witnessed the dramatic rise of Islam in Indonesian society and the state. By this time, three decades of sustained economic growth, urbanization, and the extension of the tertiary educational sector had brought into the ranks of the educated urban middle class an unprecedented number of Muslims coming from pious backgrounds. This trend was evident in the growing prominence of devout, mostly modernist, Muslims in the business world, on university campuses, in the mass media, and, increasingly, in the armed forces, the bureaucracy, and other power centers within the state—preserves previously dominated by Christians and secularized Muslims.

The creation of the All-Indonesian Association of Islamic Intellectuals (Ikatan Cendekiawan Muslimin se-Indonesia or ICMI) in 1990 worked to recognize and reinforce this trend. With Suharto's long-time close associate B. J. Habibie as its chairman, ICMI came to serve as an important network for recruitment into the political class and as a generously endowed source of patronage. Under its auspices, moreover, support for "Muslim professionals" was accompanied by promotion of "professional Muslims," through ICMI backing for a diverse range of Islamic publishing, preaching, and associational activities. Embedded within the authoritarian state, and enjoying unprecedented and unparalleled opportunities for state promotion of Islam, ICMI gave great sustenance and hope to those Islamic activists concerned with overcoming Indonesia's famously diverse Islamic practices and associations, and with promoting a modernist, reified notion of Islam. Thus the resignation of Suharto and the immediate assumption of the presidency by then–vice president Habibie in May 1998 represented the triumph of the "Islamic trend" in Indonesia (Hefner 1993; Liddle 1996).

With the elections of June 1999, however, the fiction of a united Muslim population, represented by Habibie and his allied forces, dissipated with fragmentation and factionalism among a welter of Islamic parties, and dissolved in the face of strong

> **With the elections of June 1999...the fiction of a united Muslim population...dissolved**

electoral showings by non-Islamist parties among Muslim and non-Muslim

John T. Sidel

voters alike. Indeed, in the 1999 elections a clear plurality of the vote (34 percent) was won by Megawati Soekarnoputri's Indonesian Democratic Party of Struggle (Partai Demokrasi Indonesia—Perjuangan or PDI-P), a party known for its Soekarnoist lineages, secular-nationalist, ecumenical, and syncretist orientation, and sizable non-Muslim constituencies and membership. More than one-third of the members of parliament elected on the PDI-P ticket were non-Muslims (mostly Protestants), and virtually none of its Muslim MPs claimed a background of Islamic education or associational activity.[3] By contrast, parties with avowedly Islamic agendas and affiliations—Partai Persatuan Pembangunan (United Development Party), Partai Bulan Bintang (Crescent Star Party), and Partai Keadilan (Justice Party)—achieved less than 20 percent of the vote, with the Partai Amanat Nasional (National Mandate Party), led by the modernist Muslim association Muhammadiyah's chairman Amien Rais, winning 8 percent under an ostensibly ecumenical banner and with token non-Muslims in its ranks. The universalistic claims made under the sign of Islam were fully revealed as partisan, particularistic, and rather poorly received even among the broad mass of the Muslim population.

Islamic parties avoided frank admission of defeat in the aftermath of the June 1999 elections thanks only to the peculiarities of Indonesia's inherited, early post-authoritarian system for indirect election of the president by the People's Consultative Assembly (Majelis Permusyawaratan Rakyat or MPR) in October of the same year. A group of Islamic parties known as the Central Axis (Poros Tengah) cobbled together a coalition in the MPR to defeat the candidacy of PDI-P chairwoman Megawati Soekarnoputri and to elect long-time Nahdlatul Ulama (NU) chairman and National Awakening Party (Partai Kebangkitan Bangsa or PKB) leader Abdurrahman Wahid as president instead. But Wahid was quick to turn on his erstwhile supporters, removing from his cabinet or otherwise marginalizing ministers associated with the various Islamic parties. He also centralized power in the hands of close associates, including family members, drawn from traditionalist NU circles and from the ranks of the secularized, liberal Muslim and Christian groups with which he had long allied himself and NU. Long associated with the promotion of religious tolerance, Wahid was especially concerned about the protection of Indonesia's minority faiths and extremely opposed to other Muslim leaders' efforts to rally public support for *jihad* in the provinces of Maluku and North Maluku and in the Central Sulawesi regency of Poso, where interreligious violence had claimed hundreds if not thousands of Muslim and Christian lives. Thus the same Central Axis parties' leaders who had publicly rejoiced at the election of a prominent Muslim figure to the presidency soon spoke about Wahid's betrayal of their trust and support and began maneuvering to promote the early demise of his presidency. In mid-2000 and again in mid-2001, these Muslim parties and other anti-Wahid forces used the occasion of the Annual Session of the People's Consultative Assembly first to censure the president, and then to compel his early removal from office (Van Dijk 2001: 431–534).

In short, the onset of *jihad* in early to mid-2000 was the result of disappointment if not despair about the precipitous reversal of the gains Islam had achieved in the 1990s. The country's new president and most prominent Muslim leader, after all, was no longer an ally of Islamist forces but instead a representative of Indonesian Islam known to be comfortable and cooperative with Western liberal, Christian, Javanist, and secular elements in Indonesia and beyond (see, for example, *Suara Hidayatullah* 2000). Beyond the narrow realm of formal politics, moreover, the processes of democratization and decentralization unfolding since 1999 gave rise to manifold alternative interpellations—by spokesmen for *adat* (customary law), for aristocratic claims to traditional authority, for various ethnic identities and loyalties, for indigenous peoples, and for a variety of local and national causes—that crosscut and competed with the articulation of claims in the name of Islam (Davidson and Henley 2007). Against this backdrop, the atrocities committed by armed Christian groups against Muslim communities in various parts of Maluku and North Maluku in the final week of December 1999 and the first week of January 2000 signaled the apparent obliviousness and apathy of the Wahid administration, the mainstream media, and the Muslim population in the face of threats and indignities to Islam.

It was thus not only to assist vulnerable co-religionists in areas of interfaith conflict, but also to reassert and reawaken seemingly lapsed religious sensibilities and solidarities, that a call for *jihad* was issued by prominent Islamist politicians and activists in the early months of 2000. The response to this call assumed the form of paramilitary training and mobilization by forces identified with Islamist organizations within the broad family of Persatuan Islam, Al-Irsyad, and Dewan Dakwah Islamiyah Indonesia (DDII). Most prominent was the formation of Laskar Jihad by

Ja'far Umar Thalib, a graduate of Al-Irsyad and Persatuan Islam schools who had studied in Pakistan on a DDII scholarship and had briefly joined the *mujahidin* on the border with Afghanistan. Under Thalib's leadership, and with the connivance of sympathetic elements in the armed forces, a few thousand young activists undertook paramilitary training in camps on Java in early 2000, and were subsequently deployed to Maluku as early as May of that year (Hasan 2006). Although this initial phase of *jihad* expanded to Poso in July 2001, conditions in Indonesia and beyond spelled its termination and transformation in subsequent months.

Indeed, mid-2001 witnessed not only a massacre of Laskar Jihad troops by security forces in the Maluku provincial capital city of Ambon, but also further defeats for Islam in Jakarta. The Central Axis parties had failed to prevent the election of the PDI-P's Megawati Soekarnoputri to the vice presidency in 1999, and this position, the strength of her party's contingent in parliament, and her close connections to elements in the military establishment combined to make her the eventual replacement for Wahid in July 2001. While the Central Axis had worked assiduously against a Megawati presidency in 1999, raising doubts about her Muslim faith and about the suitability of a woman as president in light of Islamic doctrine, by mid-2001 the leaders of these parties were climbing on board the bandwagon that would bring her to the palace. Hamzah Haz, the chairman of the United Development Party (Partai Persatuan Pembangunan or PPP), agreed to serve as Megawati's vice president, and representatives of other Islamist parties accepted seats in the new cabinet (Slater 2004).

This acquiescence in the elevation of Megawati to the presidency came at a considerable price. First of all, it served as a public acknowledgment of the real limits to Islamist advancement through parliamentary party politics. By 2001, after all, the various Islamic parties had essentially given up on their avowed efforts to insert key phrases about Islamic law into the Constitution. Within each Islamic party, this co-optation and cooperation with the Megawati administration gave rise to considerable grumbling— and threats of rebellion—from less well-connected and conciliatory elements, but the accommodationists prevailed.

In addition, the co-optation of the various Muslim parties by 2001 allowed Megawati to pursue the kind of ecumenical, secular nationalist agenda with which the PDI-P had long been identified. At the same time, she offered scant protection to the Islamic activists who had mobilized with these parties' encouragement—and with accompanying military protection—in the preceding years of the Habibie and Wahid administrations. Thus the months following Megawati's ascension to the presidency witnessed the continuation and escalation of the crackdown on Laskar Jihad by the security forces, leading to its forced demobilization and virtual disappearance from Maluku and Poso by early 2002 in the wake of the peace accords imposed on these two areas, the arrest of Ja'far Umar Thalib in early May, and the disbanding of the group in October of the same year (Davis 2002). *after Bali bombing.*

The networks of Muslim politicians, bureaucrats, businessmen, clerics, and retired and active police and military officers who had mobilized to support their co-religionists in Maluku and Poso faced a broader campaign of government harassment and intimidation as well. Most prominent in this regard was the well-publicized arrest and imprisonment in Manila in March 2002 of three Indonesian Muslim activists on clearly trumped-up charges of smuggling explosives, a move allegedly made by the Philippine authorities at the urging of the new head of the Indonesian National Intelligence Agency (BIN), (Ret.) Lt. Gen. A. M. Hendropriyono, a close associate of Megawati. Among the three activists was the national treasurer of both Amien Rais's party Partai Amanat Nasional (PAN) and of DDII, who was also a leading figure in a DDII-sponsored group, KOMPAK (Komite Aksi Penanggulangan Akibat Krisis, or Crisis Response Action Committee), which was active in its support of *jihad* in Maluku and Poso. Also arrested was the deputy head of the South Sulawesi branch of PAN, a fellow KOMPAK activist who also served as the leader of a South Sulawesi group calling for the implementation of Islamic law, and as the founder of a group of armed Muslim fighters (Laskar Jundullah) active in Poso (Linrung 2003).

Following arrests made in Malaysia, the Philippines, and Singapore in early 2002, a religious school in Ngruki, a small hamlet on the outskirts of the Central Javanese city of Solo, was identified as a center of recruitment for alleged Islamist terrorist activists. Affiliated with the puritanical tradition of Al-Irsyad and Persatuan Islam, and associated with DDII, this *pesantren* was alleged to be at the center of a "Ngruki network" of Islamist terrorist activities (ICG 2002a; Soepriyadi 2003; Qodir 2003). K. H. Abu Bakar Ba'asyir, the founder of the Ngruki *pesantren* and, as of August 2000, the elected head of the Indonesian Assembly of Holy Warriors (Majelis

gov't crack-down

Mujahidin Indonesia), was called in for questioning by the police in early 2002 and arrested later the same year (*Tempo* 2002b: 20–22; 2002c: 20–22; 2002d: 24–26; 2002e: 30).

It was thus only in the midst of a domestic and international crackdown on Islamist activists in Indonesia that a bombing campaign against Western targets began to unfold in late 2002, beginning in Bali (October 2002) and recurring at the Marriott Hotel (August 2003) the Australian Embassy in Jakarta (September 2004), and restaurants catering to tourists in Bali (October 2005). As noted above, the inauguration and entrenchment of the Megawati administration in mid-2001 spelled the decline and defeat, if not effective disappearance, of the Islamist project in Indonesian parliamentary politics, while accompanying social trends worked to undermine efforts to strengthen religious solidarities among Muslims. Even as the new government in Jakarta appeared to prioritize the promotion of Chinese business and the protection of Protestant communities—and PDI-P politicians—in Maluku and Poso through peace accords, a crackdown on Laskar Jihad and other Muslim paramilitary forces, and religiously coded gerrymandering in these areas, the complicity of Muslim politicians, and the complacency of the Muslim population at large were amply apparent.

Meanwhile, the onset of the Global War on Terrorism in the aftermath of the September 11, 2001 attacks on New York City and Washington, D.C. soon encouraged the pursuit of Muslim fighters involved in the *jihad* in Maluku and Poso and the persecution and prosecution of Islamic activists supporting their struggle. As early as November 2001, for example, U.S. deputy defense secretary Paul Wolfowitz, a leading hawk in the Bush administration and a former ambassador to Jakarta, warned that "going after Al-Qaeda in Indonesia is not something that should wait until after Al-Qaeda has been uprooted from Afghanistan" (*Far Eastern Economic Review* 2001: 22–23; *Tempo Interaktif* 2001). Allegations that Al-Qaeda had established training camps in Poso, enjoyed connections to *mujahidin* in Ambon, and forged links with Abu Bakar Ba'asyir and Jemaah Islamiyah were soon issued by high-ranking foreign officials, reported in the Indonesian media, and acted upon by the military, police, intelligence, and judiciary arms of the Megawati administration. In

> *American pressure expedited...a crackdown on the networks of jihadi fighters and conspirators*

tandem with widely publicized arrests and accusations by authorities in neighboring Malaysia, the Philippines, and Singapore eager to demonstrate their commitment to the Global War on Terrorism, American pressure expedited and escalated a crackdown on the networks of *jihadi* fighters and conspirators that had emerged and expanded in Indonesia in the preceding years.

In short, the shift of the form and focus of Islamist violence, from paramilitary mobilization in areas of interreligious conflict to the bombing of Western targets in 2002, reflected the new constellation of power relations and religious authority that had begun to crystallize at the time (*Tempo* 2001a: 60–80). The space for the promotion of Islam in the national parliamentary arena had dramatically shrunk, and the channels of quiet collaboration between *jihadi* activists and sympathetic elements in the state and the political class were rapidly being closed by powerful anti-Islamist forces in Indonesia and internationally. The banner of Islam no longer seemed to carry the potential to mobilize and unify significant numbers of Indonesian Muslims, either as crowds or as voters, or as supporters of *jihad*.

Against this political, sociological, and discursive backdrop, the internationalization of the bombing campaign represented the extrusion of the internal contradictions and the limitations of the Islamist project in Indonesia, with externalization forestalling if not foreclosing a belated acknowledgment and acceptance of decline and defeat. This attempt to restore the visibility and viability of Islam at the moment of its relegation to a minor, compromised role within Indonesia's emerging oligarchic democracy coincided with the rise to global prominence of Al-Qaeda and Osama bin Laden and the retaliatory Global War on Terrorism, which accorded foreign, and especially Western, targets special priority and prestige. Yet the specific timing, locations, protagonists, and forms of *jihad* reflected the peculiarities of Indonesian conditions.

The significance of the Indonesian political, sociological, and discursive context is especially apparent when preceding episodes of *jihad* in recent Indonesian history are considered, including both the paramilitary mobilization associated with the Darul Islam (Abode of Islam) movement of the 1950s and early 1960s and the bombing campaigns of the mid-1980s. The proclamation of the Negara Islam Indonesia (Islamic State of Indonesia) in mid-1949, after all, represented a break with the conciliatory stance of republican leaders during the revolution against Dutch colonial rule by a group of Muslim independence fighters led by S. M. Kartosoewirjo, a protégé of the founder of Sarekat Islam and a one-time associate of Soekarno. With independence, the favoritism shown toward graduates of secular schools in the staffing of the Indonesian state (including the army), the forced demobilization of the irregular guerrilla groups that had contributed so much energy to the revolution, the rejection of special provisions for Islam and Islamic law in the Constitution in favor of the multifaith (but monotheistic) Pancasila, and the growing divisions among Muslims that accompanied constitutional democracy all contributed to a rising sense of disappointment and disenchantment among those who had mobilized against the Dutch under the banner of Islam. Thus the early 1950s saw the emergence of the Darul Islam (Abode of Islam) movement, with armed guerrilla groups from the revolution mobilized against the embryonic Indonesian state as late as the early 1960s in provinces such as West Java, South Sulawesi, South Kalimantan, and Aceh and some northern coastal towns of Central Java (Horikoshi 1975; Van Dijk 1981; Soebardi 1983).

This early episode of *jihad* in reaction to the decline and defeat of a previously ascendant Islam in Indonesia recurred in the form of a bombing campaign in the 1980s, during the peak years of non-Muslim and anti-Islamist influence in the Suharto era. The early to mid-1980s witnessed a set of humiliating defeats for forces identified with the promotion of Islam in Indonesia, as well as the simultaneous ascension of Christians—and Catholics in particular—to the leadership of the armed forces, key cabinet posts, and other positions of power within the regime. After the strong performance of the Islamic party PPP in the 1977 and 1982 parliamentary elections, the authoritarian Suharto regime embarked on a campaign to defang the threat of a populist Islam. This campaign included the imposition of more subservient pro-government figures within the PPP leadership, the promotion of the liberal accommodationist Abdurrahman Wahid as the new chairman of NU, the encouragement of Wahid's withdrawal of NU support for PPP, and the passage of legislation insisting that all organizations accept Pancasila—rather than, say, Islam—as their guiding principles. As this campaign proceeded in the early to mid-1980s, it provoked violent reactions in the name of Islam. This reaction was first evident in an attack on a local police station by residents of the Jakarta port area of Tanjung Priok in September 1984, but the resulting massacre by the security forces in Tanjung Priok was followed by a subsequent wave of government repression and apparent Islamist reprisals. Even as Muslim preachers and other activists accused of inciting violence in Tanjung Priok and elsewhere in the country were arrested, imprisoned, and put on trial in late 1984 and early 1985, a series of bombings took place around the Indonesian archipelago. These bombs targeted diverse sites of non-Muslim power and influence: a Chinese-owned bank and a Chinese-owned shopping mall in Jakarta in October 1984; a Catholic church and a Protestant seminary elsewhere on Java on Christmas Eve of the same year; the world-famous ruins of the pre-Islamic kingdom of Sailendra in Borobodur, Central Java, in January 1985; and a tourist bus bound for Bali in March of the same year (Tapol 1987: 71–87).

In light of the Darul Islam rebellions of the 1950s and early 1960s and the bombings of the early to mid-1980s, the terrorist bombings in Indonesia of recent years thus appear less as the product of (essentially exogenous) Wahhabi or Salafi influence, Afghanistan experience, or Al-Qaeda outreach than as the most recent variation on a recurring theme in Indonesian history. The activists recruited for *jihad* in Maluku and Poso in 2000–01 and for bombings around the country in 2002–05, after all, seem to have been drawn from the very same networks involved in the Darul Islam movement of the 1950s and the bombing campaign of the mid-1980s. Yet these networks, it should be stressed, do not appear to have been involved in any form of religious violence in Indonesia in the intervening decades, which were free of armed insurgencies and terrorist bombing campaigns. Their engagement in full-time, full-blown terrorist *jihad* came only under certain specific circumstances: in the wake of rising popular mobilization and increasingly assertive claims on the public sphere and the state articulated in the idiom of Islam, and during a period of decline, defeat, disappointment, and disentanglement from state power for those forces most closely associated with the promotion of the faith. Thus the Islamist terrorism of recent years in Indonesia should be understood not as evidence of an ascendant, insurgent Islam but as a symptom of the weakness of those who have tried to mobilize in its name, with both sore losers and ungracious winners involved in its perpetration.

Indonesia: Waning Islamist Unity and Influence in the Public Sphere

If this is the case, what, then, of the broader pattern of Islamist activity, influence, and assertiveness that is so often described in alarmist terms as constituting a broader Islamist threat in Indonesia? What about the continuing influence and assertiveness of Islamist forces in Indonesian society, in national politics, and in the formulation and implementation of government policies? What about the aggression and intimidation attributed to Islamist vigilante groups and the imposition of Islamic law in localities dominated by Islamist parties?

Compared to the apogee of Islamist influence and access to power under the brief administration of B. J. Habibie (May 1998–October 1999), recent years have witnessed the diminution, demobilization, and domestication of Islamist forces in Indonesia. As suggested above, this shift is evident if one considers the failed efforts of Islamist parties in 1999–2002 to insert references to Islamic law into the Constitution, and the subsequent acquiescence of these parties in the reaffirmation of the ecumenical, if insistently monotheistic, principles of Pancasila as the parameters of social and political life in the country (Hosen 2005). This shift is likewise apparent if one compares the prominence and power of modernist and puritanical strains in Indonesian Islam in 1998–99 with the subsequent political triumphs of traditionalist Muslim, ecumenical, and even Christian elements in political contests in Jakarta, and with broader societal trends. Indeed, the past several years have seen the flourishing of diverse forms of religious expression and associational activity within

> *[Recent] years have seen the flourishing of diverse forms of religious expression...within Indonesian Islam*

Indonesian Islam, which is famous for its diversity, its organizational pluralism, its syncretic tendencies, and its engagement with the secularizing forces of the capitalist market and the modern state. Journalists have tracked the rising popularity of Sufi brotherhoods and of diverse religious cults, both in Jakarta and other major cities and in the rural hinterlands of the archipelago (Howell 2001; *Tempo* 2006g: 54–55). The past few years have also witnessed the rise of new charismatic *kyai* who enjoy unprecedented popularity outside established Islamic associational hierarchies, thanks to the appeal of their mystical, Sufistic, and "supernatural" approaches (*Tempo* 2006s: 100–109). Meanwhile, unofficial religious groups that have long existed on the fringes of the permissible have begun to press for more official recognition of their de facto authority over sizable flocks of the faithful (*Tempo* 2006q: 44–45; 2006r: 46). Scholars tracing these trends have written of the increasing "permeability in the boundaries of the nation's official religions," and the "emergence of an arena of unregulated 'spiritual' groups that now exists along the highly regulated, rigidly denominational religious market structured by the New Order Government (1996–98)" (Howell 2005: 473). Overall, the existing hierarchies of Islamic worship and learning in Indonesia are today facing unprecedented difficulties in maintaining their authority over the diverse population of 200 million Muslims across the archipelago.

Meanwhile, the unfolding of political and social liberalization, democratization, and decentralization in the years since the fall of Suharto in 1998, as well as the economic recovery and growth experienced in the aftermath of the deep financial crisis of the same year, have drawn millions of Indonesians into forms of identity, activity, and association that compete with those offered by Islam. Thus recent years have seen the revival of ethnic and regional identities, the reemergence of *adat* (customary law) and aristocratic lineages in local politics, and a modest resurgence of labor activism, all at the expense of efforts to promote a streamlined, standardized, universalistic Islam. Meanwhile, against these centrifugal tendencies toward fragmentation along regional, ethnic, and class lines, the centripetal force of the revitalized Indonesian economy has continued to attract millions of Indonesian Muslims to forms of consumption—of clothing, technology, and entertainment—that also work to pull them away from religious piety. Under conditions of unprecedented liberalization, the Indonesian entertainment industry—from movies to radio and television soap operas, romance novels, and pop music—is highly vibrant today, a producer of domestic content and a transmitter of global popular culture.

It is in this context that the efforts of various Islamist politicians and parties to reassert their power and influence in public life in Indonesia must be situated. The quasi-governmental Council of Indonesian Islamic Scholars (Majelis Ulama Indonesia or MUI), for example, has in recent years issued a series of controversial *fatwa* (Arabic: sing. *fatwā*; pl. *fatāwā*), including one condemning "pluralism, secularism, and liberalism" and another denouncing as heretical the Ahmadiyah sect (Bowen 2003; Ichwan 2005; *Jakarta Post* 2005a; *Kompas* 2005). But these *fatwa* are neither legally binding nor representative of the elected government's policies and preferences (Hooker 2003). Indeed, the issuance of these *fatwa* has provoked considerable controversy in the Indonesian press, with prominent Islamic figures such as former president and Nahdlatul Ulama chairman Abdurrahman Wahid condemning the edicts and calling for the abolition of the MUI.

While alarmist accounts cite the MUI *fatwa* as evidence of mounting Islamist assertiveness and intolerance, there is ample reason to think otherwise. After all, they were issued under a consolidated Indonesian democracy, in which pluralism is alive and well, not only in terms of political parties competing for public offices, but also in the realm of religious associational, educational, and devotional life. These *fatwa* were issued against the backdrop of a recovering Indonesian economy, whose deepening integration into global markets has been accompanied by the increasing availability and consumption of images, products, and services whose origins are utterly secular in nature. They were also issued during a period of ongoing liberalization of Indonesian society, a period in which individual freedoms were expanding in all realms of social life. Finally, the *fatwa* were issued by a body lacking in official juridical authority or capacity for enforcement, a body forced to compete for Muslim hearts and minds with newly formed groups like the Liberal Islam Network (Jaringan Islam Liberal or JIL), whose activities and publications are generously funded by U.S.-based foundations.

Another oft-cited example of Islamist assertiveness and intolerance in Indonesia is efforts to restrict the public visibility and freedom of women in the country. The publication of a new Indonesian edition of Playboy magazine in April 2006, for example, was met by vehement condemnation in the press—and angry protests in the streets—by various Islamist groups, even though the editors had decided not to include nude centerfolds or other photos of naked women as had originally been anticipated (*New York Times* 2006b). Early 2006 also saw the eruption of controversy over legislation proposed by Islamist parties ostensibly to restrict pornography in Indonesia, but which in fact introduced broad regulations on women's dress and behavior in public (*Tempo* 2006a: 76–77). Alongside the controversy over this proposed legislation, which remains under consideration by a parliamentary committee as of this writing, came well-publicized attacks by Islamist groups against a highly popular Indonesian dancer, whose allegedly sensual gyrations had earned her considerable live and video audiences, and whose string of cafes and nightclubs in Jakarta had attracted a growing clientele (*Tempo* 2006b: 34–35; *Asia Times* 2006a).

While alarmist accounts of growing Islamist influence cite these episodes as evidence of increasing encroachment on the freedoms of women in Indonesia, a more balanced assessment of the situation suggests otherwise. As many authors have noted, Islamist groups in diverse settings have long been preoccupied with the exercise of social control over women, treating them, in the words of the eminent Middle East specialist Charles Tripp, "as the terrain for the symbolic expression of a certain kind of Islamic identity, but also as key players in the defence against the intrusion of other belief systems" (Tripp 2006: 168). As Tripp further notes:

> Echoing contemporary secular nationalist discourses, there is stress on the functional role of women in maintaining and reproducing a distinctively Islamic society, through the act of giving birth and educating children. The security of the domestic environment becomes the guarantee of a truly Islamic society, since it is the site for the production of the strong "Islamic personality" who does battle with the world in the service of Islamic values. This places a heavy historical and sociological responsibility on women, making their comportment and actions a matter for general concern by the largely male cohort of concerned Muslim intellectuals. (Ibid.: 168–69)

Indeed, in Indonesia the issue of Muslim women's attire had long been a focus of Islamist activists' attention and political agitation, most notably in the late 1980s and early 1990s, when the government's long-standing prohibition on Islamic headscarves in state schools was overturned in favor of permissiveness and encouragement (Brenner 1996; *Surabaya Post* 1991a; 1991b).

This Islamist concern with restricting and regulating women's behavior in public life must be understood in the context of the increasing mobility of women in Indonesian society in recent decades (Brenner 2005; Smith-Hefner 2005). Already in the Suharto era, economic growth, industrialization, and urbanization had brought millions of Indonesian women out of the homes and villages of the country and into factory belts, supermarkets and department stores, and, in smaller numbers, universities, opening up a range of urban professional opportunities up to them (Wolf

1992; Bennett 2005). With recovery from the economic crisis of 1997–98, these trends have resumed in the post-Suharto era. With every passing year, more Indonesian women are traveling farther from home, working in industrial and service jobs, joining the ranks of the civil service and the professional classes, and exercising more choice over their movements, the use of their labor power and their money, and their modes of communication and expression than ever before (Blackburn 2001; Sen 2005). The creation of the Ministry for the Empowerment of Women represents the government's belated recognition of—and reaction to—these trends, even as the growing ranks and range of activities of women's organizations attached to Muhammadiyah and Nahdlatul Ulama attest to the accommodating response of mainstream Islamic groups in Indonesia (Van Doorn-Harder 2003).

women's rights

Other trends have worked to undermine the conservative understandings of family life and sexuality assiduously promoted by the Suharto regime during the three decades of its reign (Suryakusuma 1996). Homosexuality is more visible in the public sphere than ever before, as perhaps best exemplified by the book launch for a novel about a lesbian love affair held at a branch of the State Islamic Institute (Institut Agama Islam Negeri or IAIN) in late 2003 (Boellstorff 2004; 2005a; 2005b). As Dédé Oetomo, Indonesia's best-known openly gay public figure, has noted, there is "a greatly increased public awareness of the variety of human sexualities. . . . True, many misunderstandings remain, but they are eroding" (Oetomo 2001). Small wonder that male Islamist activists—and other men anxious about the weakening hold of conservative patterns of familial authority and gender relations—have tried to reassert various forms of control over sexuality in public life in Indonesia.

PKS

These efforts to shore up conservative notions of propriety and rectitude in Indonesian social life have in some measure been matched in the political realm, with the much-ballyhooed rise to prominence—and influence—of the Prosperous Justice Party (Partai Keadilan Sejahtera or PKS). The party won more than 7 percent of the vote in the 2004 parliamentary elections, placing it above the established National Mandate Party (PAN) of former Muhammadiyah chairman Amien Rais and just behind current president Susilo Bambang Yudhoyono's Democratic Party (Partai Demokrat), with especially strong showings in Jakarta and other major Indonesian cities. Today, former PKS chairman Hidayat Nur Wahid serves as the head of the supra-parliamentary People's Consultative Assembly

(Majelis Permusyawaratan Rakyat or MPR), the party is well represented in local assemblies, and PKS-backed candidates have fared well in recent elections for local executive posts as mayors, regents, and governors around the country. Some party activists and other political analysts predict even greater successes for the PKS in the 2009 national elections (*International Herald Tribune* 2004a, 2004b).

Like many other political parties in the Muslim world identifying themselves as supporting justice, prosperity, and welfare, Indonesia's PKS is decidedly Islamist in its origins and orientation. Its leadership emerged out of a network of highly pious, puritanical, and politicized university students that evolved over the course of the Suharto era, linking discussion groups from various campus mosques in the country's top universities as well as Indonesian Muslim students at universities in the Middle East and elsewhere in the world. Even as they pursued doctorates in various technical and scientific fields, these students were attracted to puritanical currents in Islamic thinking and to the organizational and mobilizational techniques developed by Hasan Al-Banna and the Muslim Brotherhood in Egypt since the 1930s (Damanik 2000; Furkon 2004).

While the PKS's emergence and orientation may remind readers of similar—and often similarly named—Islamist parties and movements elsewhere in the Muslim world, whether in Pakistan, Turkey, Egypt, or Morocco, the party's actual modus operandi, from election campaigning to parliamentary coalition building, is reminiscent of the pattern of co-optation, domestication, and transformation of such Islamist parties noted by many observers (Langohr 2001; Wiktorowicz 2001; Mecham 2004; Clark 2006; Schwedler 2006). The party's appeal among voters, after all, came not from its commitment to the Islamization of Indonesian state and society, but from a reputation for relative incorruptibility and seriousness of purpose compared to the prevailing corruption and machine politics in the country. The nature of this appeal has been evident not only in the party's official name and policy pronouncements, but also in its campaign rallies, which have attracted thousands of clean-shaven men and headscarf-less women, as the author observed firsthand in both Bandung and Jakarta in the weeks leading up to the 2004 parliamentary elections. After the 2004 elections and the inauguration of the administration of Susilo Bambang Yudhoyono, this emphasis on fighting corruption in PKS public relations was evident in the resignation of Hidayat Nur Wahid from the party leadership prior to his elevation to speaker of the MPR, in the party's MPs' rejection of many of the perks of parliamentary office, and in the party's avowedly principled— rather than patronage-based—support for the new president's choice of cabinet ministers (*Tempo Interaktif* 2004, 2005; *Pikiran Rakyat* 2005).

Skeptics and alarmists see the public profile of the PKS as a thin veneer behind which the "fundamentalists" running the party have succeeded in luring unsuspecting voters into support for the party and in lulling other politicians into complacency as the party consolidates its gains and expands its influence. They claim the party's public disavowal of intentions to seek Islamist amendments to the Constitution, its inclusion of many women and token non-Muslims among its internal governing bodies and parliamentary slates, and other efforts to deemphasize the party's Islamist origins and orientation are simply duplicitous (*Tempo* 2005c, 2005e, 2006d). Once the party expands its share of the electorate and its influence in parliament and the cabinet, the PKS will show its true colors and reveal itself for the extremist, intolerant, fundamentalist party they believe it remains at heart (*The Nation* 2005).

Yet what this alarmist interpretation of PKS ignores is the extent to which the party's participation within the parliamentary arena has transformed if not its leaders' conscious sense of commitment to long-term Islamist goals, then their unconscious understanding of the party's short- and medium-term interests *as well as its very identity*. For whatever the PKS leaders may confide amongst themselves, their continuing efforts to promote the party as the vehicle of essentially secular good governance have reoriented the party's collective activities, its style and language of self-presentation, and its members' everyday practices in a not particularly Islamist direction. Meanwhile, as the party has engaged in informal, behind-the-scenes horse-trading and coalition building with machine politicians of various stripes over recent years, its effective commitment to various high-minded goals—whether good governance or Islam—has been compromised. Thus, like the Christian Democrats in Western Europe before World War I, and the Euro-Communists during the Cold War, the Islamists of today may

> ### Islamists...may well be duping themselves more than they are duping others

well be duping themselves more than they are duping others, with parties such as Indonesia's PKS effectively embodying gradual Islamist integration and accommodation, willy-nilly, with liberal democracy (Roy 2004: 72–83; Nasr 2005; Kalyvas 1996). Compared to other Islamist parties in the Muslim world, moreover, the PKS seems to lack the kind of densely woven and deeply rooted local infrastructure so carefully nurtured over the years by their counterparts in Egypt, Jordan, Turkey, Pakistan, the Gaza Strip, and the West Bank.

This weakness is readily apparent if one considers local politics in Indonesia, which in recent years has been described in alarmist terms as dominated by aggressive Islamic vigilante groups and initiatives to impose Islamic law. The impression imparted is one of widespread Islamist activism at the local level throughout Indonesia, with accumulating Islamist momentum "from below" around the country under conditions of decentralization since the enactment of "regional autonomy" legislation in 1999. For example, from its formation in mid-1998 during the brief Habibie interlude to this day, the Front for the Defenders of Islam (Front Pembela Islam or FPI) has won considerable media attention for its high-profile campaigns against gambling, prostitution, and alcohol in Jakarta and other cities, its occasional anti-U.S. protests, and its antics as an enforcer of Islamic morality (*Gatra* 2006c; *Tempo* 2006h: 26–28). The year 2005 saw a series of widely publicized attacks by FPI and other Islamist groups that coalesced into an "anti-apostasy movement" against churches in West Java accused of operating without licenses and attempting to spread Christianity among the Muslim population (*Sinar Indonesia Baru* 2005; *Tempo* 2005d; *Jakarta Post* 2005b). Finally, by 2006 press coverage of local politics in Indonesia had begun to focus on the supposedly growing number of regencies where local assemblies had imposed regulations in the name of Islamic law, banning gambling, prostitution, and alcohol, for example, or imposing restrictions on women's dress and comportment in public (*Tempo* 2006j: 62–65; 2006k: 66–67). In the province of South Sulawesi alone, at least six of twenty-four regencies were cited as localities where various forms of *shari'a* law were in place (*Gatra* 2006a: 20–24; 2006b: 25–26; *Tempo* 2006d: 26–28; 2006e: 30; 2006f: 33; International Crisis Group 2006b). The case of a young woman detained for alleged "prostitution" in the Jakarta suburb of Tangerang for being improperly clad while awaiting an evening bus home from work similarly attracted national and international publicity (*Tempo* 2006c: 30–31; *New York Times* 2006a).

Here again, this alarmist picture of widespread Islamist activism, aggression, and influence—and of the increasing imposition of Islamic law—around the Indonesian archipelago is highly exaggerated and distorted, obscuring the broader trends at work in local politics. Indeed, compared to the preceding decade, the most striking feature of local politics in Indonesia is the relative absence of violence: nothing like the anti-Chinese riots of 1995–97, the widespread mayhem of 1998, or the incidents of communal violence of 1999–2001 has occurred over the past several years (*Tempo* 2006m: 84–86; 2006n: 88–89; 2006p: 90–91). Even in the Central Sulawesi regency of Poso or the provinces of Maluku and Maluku Utara, where interreligious violence caused a few thousand deaths in

> *the most striking feature of local politics in Indonesia is the relative absence of violence*

1999–2001, there has been virtually no resurgence of large-scale communal conflict. Indeed, the rising incidence of church burnings documented by concerned Christian groups in the 1990s tapered off and has virtually ceased since the turn of the twenty-first century. Overall, accommodation between Muslims and non-Muslims is the norm in local politics, as evident in the success of the ecumenical parties Golkar and PDI-P in the majority of local parliamentary elections and the prevalence of interreligious coalitions in the elections for local executive posts.

To be sure, Islamic parties such as PKS have come to enjoy considerable popularity and influence in certain locations around the country, regional assemblies dominated by Islamist parties have enacted *shari'a* regulations in a number of locations, and groups like FPI exert informal forms of influence and intimidation in the name of Islam. Yet some caveats are in order. First of all, as suggested above, the areas—and episodes—of Islamist activism are hardly representative of a general trend in the vast majority of localities around the vast Indonesian archipelago, with its majority-Muslim population of 225 million people. Second, insofar as the PKS and other Islamic forces have enjoyed some success in local politics in recent years, it is far from clear that this trend should be viewed solely with trepidation. After all, the basis of the local appeal of PKS—and the focus of its local campaign energies—has been its struggle against local corruption, as embodied in the machine politics dominated by the two largest ecumenical parties, Golkar and PDI-P (Henderson and Kuncoro 2006). In many provinces, moreover, alongside the PKS and other Islamic parties, Islamic university student organizations and other Islamic associational networks have provided virtually the only effective counterweight in civil society to the vast patronage resources and regulatory powers of the state (Collins 2004). Third and finally, it seems clear that not all Islamist politics should be taken so seriously in ideological terms: groups like FPI and their backers and collaborators have used the threat of violence in the name of Islam for extortionate purposes, and local assemblies' enactment of so-called *shari'a* legislation has likewise served to expand the regulatory powers of the local state, the discretionary privileges of local politicians, and the rent-seeking opportunities of local enforcers. Even in South Sulawesi, where the spread of local *shari'a* regulations appears to be most advanced, knowledgeable observers report that Islamist parties and politicians remain involved in all manner of opportunistic horse-trading and collusion with their non-Islamist counterparts in Golkar and PDI-P (Juhannis 2006). In short, the standard picture of aggressive Islamist forces on the ascendant in Indonesia in recent years is not only exaggerated and sensationalist, but it fundamentally misrepresents of the overall direction of social and political trends towards the incorporation, domestication, and transformation of Islamists within the democratization, decentralization, and liberalization of public life, and the diversification of religious practices and affiliations in Indonesia. As suggested above, the Islamist mobilization and occasional episodes of Islamist violence observed in recent years reflect a *reaction* against these prevailing trends in Indonesia rather than signs of an Islamist trend itself.

Malaysia: Contested Official Islam and the Rise and Decline of PAS

Beyond Indonesia, the world's most populous Muslim country, other Muslim areas of Southeast Asia represent similar but somewhat different cases of exaggerated Islamist threats despite the fact that the real possibilities for promoting Islam have in fact diminished considerably over the past decade. These parallels are evident if we consider the cases of Malaysia, the southern Philippines, and southern Thailand, taking account of the notable differences between the three areas.

In Malaysia, for example, the Islamist rise and decline from the 1990s to the present parallels the Indonesian trajectory, albeit in less dramatic fashion, given the relative lack of political dynamism (not to mention regime change) in the country and the greater institutionalization of Islam within the orbit of state power. Throughout the 1980s and 1990s, the UMNO-led administration of Dr. Mahathir Mohamad engaged in the assiduous promotion of Islam in Malaysian public life, an effort motivated both by concerns to "out-Islamize" the Malay opposition party PAS (Parti Islam Se-Malaysia) and by the broader imperative of maintaining social control over a population experiencing rapid change under conditions of rapid economic growth (Liow 2004b). With urbanization, industrialization, and the expansion of access to higher education increasingly threatening the patterns of ethnic segregation inherited from the colonial "plural society," the borders between Malays, Chinese, and Indians threatened to "become too permeable and fuzzy, causing confusion and potential (if not actual) political and moral disorder and chaos," in the eyes of the ruling elite (Peletz 1993: 93). Thus the final decades of the twentieth century in Malaysia saw the introduction of a plethora of new regulations imposed on Muslim Malays in the name of Islam,

> *Malaysia...parallels the Indonesian trajectory*

the empowerment of new agencies to enforce these regulations, and the provision of generous funding for Islamic learning, worship, education, and outreach (Martinez 2001). Federal-level Islamization was accompanied by state-level enactment of so-called *hudud* laws concerning crimes and punishments identified with Islamic law (Faruqi 2005). Accompanying these policies was the parallel ascendancy of politicians within UMNO with Islamist sympathies. Most notable in this regard was the rise of Anwar Ibrahim, former leader of the Islamic youth group ABIM (Angkatan Belia Islam Malaysia), to the positions of finance minister and deputy prime minister, and to the status of heir apparent to long-serving prime minister and UMNO president Mahathir (Hamayotsu 2005). These trends continued the tradition of state-based efforts to absorb and control Islam in Malaysia established more than a century ago under British colonial rule.

With the unceremonious removal of Anwar Ibrahim in 1998 and his arrest and imprisonment on trumped-up charges of sodomy came a dramatic wave of Islamist mobilization against the UMNO-led regime. The 1999 elections saw a well-publicized campaign by a new party, Parti Keadilan (Justice Party), led by Anwar's wife and supporters. More importantly and impressively, it resulted in a sharp rise in votes for PAS, giving the party twenty-seven seats in the national parliament and control over the two states of Kelantan (a long-time PAS stronghold) and Terengganu. These results represented the biggest challenge launched against UMNO since PAS's strong showing in the 1969 elections, leaving Mahathir and his party heavily reliant on the backing of their non-Malay allies in the ruling National Front (Barisan Nasional) (Noor 2003).

From this high point in Islamist fortunes in Malaysia, the past several years have witnessed a modestly downward trend. The year 2000 saw a curious incident of alleged Islamist terrorism, with the obscure and previously unknown group Al-Ma'unah surfacing in an armed raid on army depots and seizing large amounts of weapons but surrendering to the government's security forces after a five-day standoff (Mohamed 2003). The following year, moreover, saw a much wider government crackdown on alleged Islamist terrorist groups, with the detention of ten Islamic activists, including several PAS members, who were alleged to be members of the previously unknown Kumpulan Mujahidin Malaysia (Malaysian Holy Warriors Group), which was said to be led by Nik Adli Nik Aziz, the thirty-four-year-old son of the leader of PAS. On September 25, 2001, just a few days after the terrorist attacks on New York and Washington, D.C., Nik Adli was arrested and detained for two years, and a further set of arrests was made in October of the same year. All in all, more than one hundred Islamic activists, including many PAS members, were detained under the draconian Internal Security Act (Human Rights Watch 2004).

In the face of these domestic and international shifts of late 2001, Islamist forces in Malaysia soon suffered a marked decline. With the post-September 11 Malaysian government crackdown on alleged Islamist terrorists came a dramatic rapprochement with the Bush administration in Washington, D.C. The U.S. government stopped applying pressure for the release of Anwar Ibrahim from prison and embraced the Mahathir regime

> *With the...Malaysian government crackdown...came a dramatic rapprochement with the Bush administration*

wholeheartedly, moving quickly to strengthen economic and security cooperation between the United States and Malaysia. The United States also invited Prime Minister Mahathir for a state visit to Washington in May 2002 (Noor 2004: 676–77). In the face of these developments, the dangers of association with Islamist terrorism pushed many Malay Muslims to distance themselves from PAS, as seen in the decision of ABIM, Anwar Ibrahim's old student organization, to endorse UMNO and the Mahathir administration. As the prominent Malaysian scholar Farish Noor concluded, "PAS was well and truly isolated and marginalized" (Ibid.: 679). Indeed, the 2004 elections saw UMNO regaining lost ground, with PAS losing many of its parliamentary seats (including the one held by the party leader), losing control over the state government of Terengganu, and barely retaining its hold over the assembly in Kelantan (Liow 2005; Moten and Mokhtar 2006).

Since that time, diverse forces have begun to promote modest efforts to reevaluate, if not reverse, the extent and nature of Islam's role in Malaysian state and society. In its one remaining stronghold, Kelantan, PAS has reportedly begun to soften its religious rhetoric and relax the implementation of regulations imposed in the name of Islam on cultural, economic, and social life in the state (*International Herald Tribune* 2005b). In its national profile, moreover, PAS has likewise begun to try to deemphasize its Islamist orientation and aims (Liow 2005a). This trend is evident in the effort to recruit non-Muslims to its ranks (and to its slate of candidates), in the inclusion of women in top party governing bodies, and in its public pronouncements on party policy as well (*The Star* 2005; *Asia Times* 2006b). Some observers have noted the emergence of reformist elements within PAS that have been pushing for a diminution of the Islamist elements of the party's platform and public profile (Liow 2006a). Pressures have reportedly grown among a group of "Young Turks" "who feel that the party badly needs a generational change to address the more complex problems arising from globalization. In their view, the purely textual, theological, and literal interpretations of the Koran would not suffice to face the new challenges in the 21st century" (Nathan 2007: 158).

Meanwhile, and perhaps more importantly, elements in Malaysia's federal government have begun to rethink some of the state's policies with regard to regulations imposed in the name of Islam. In the face of rising complaints by nongovernmental organizations and even UMNO MPs, new restrictions have been placed on the policing powers of Religious Affairs Department agents, and new guidelines for the enforcement of religious laws have been drawn up. In early 2006, the government shelved plans to enact a more conservative family law in the face of protests by prominent women activists, including the vocal feminist group Sisters in Islam (*New Straits Times* 2005a; 2005b; 2005c; 2005d; *The Sun* 2005; *International Herald Tribune* 2005a, 2006a; *Agence France Presse* 2006). Anwar Ibrahim, now released from prison and reviving his public profile and political career, has also been lending his own credentials as an Islamic activist to such efforts to question the use of state power in the name of Islam (*International Herald Tribune* 2006c).

Today, Malaysia remains a country where Islam is enshrined in the Constitution, where Muslims' daily lives are regulated in part by Islamic law, and where restrictions on religious freedom are enforced in the name of Islam (Suara Rakyat Malaysia 2006). Yet overall, Islam increasingly figures in public life in Malaysia—a country experiencing sustained rapid industrialization, urbanization, immigration, and immersion within global circuitries of production, consumption, and communication—as an instrument for maintaining state-based regulatory power and social control, rather than as a set of guiding ideals for radical social transformation. Even so, however, there are ironies and unintended consequences accompanying the expansion of Islamic law. As Michael Peletz, the author of the most detailed ethnographic account of Islamization in Malaysia, argues, "Malaysia's Islamic courts are centrally involved in producing a modern Malay

> *Malaysia remains a country where Islam is enshrined in the Constitution*

middle class composed of relatively individualized and responsive political subjects who are not beholden to potentially compromising claims and loyalties entailed in extended kinship" (Peletz 2002: 239). Peletz concludes that the institutions of Islam in Malaysia have also helped "establish the foundations for Malaysian-style modernity and civil society" by creating, ironically enough, social spaces "for the emergence and growth of sentiments, dispositions, and embryonic ideologies" that have begun to challenge and destabilize hierarchies in both society and the state (Ibid.: 278–80). Thus, the trends over the past five years in Malaysia have, if anything, begun to suggest the increasing limitations rather than the expanding possibilities of Islamization in the country.

The Philippines: Manila's Forward Movement and Muslim Responses

Meanwhile, in the Philippines, a rash of bombings in Manila and other major cities attributed to the small and shadowy Abu Sayyaf Group over the past five years has unfolded in the midst of considerable setbacks for Islamic causes in the southern provinces of the archipelago, home to a largely poor, rural, and marginalized Muslim minority (Turner 2003; International Crisis Group 2004b; Banlaoi 2007). In the early 1970s, an armed Muslim separatist movement, the Moro National Liberation Front or MNLF, emerged in Islamized areas of Mindanao and the Sulu Archipelago, and it remained active throughout the long years of the authoritarian Marcos regime (1972–86), along with a splinter group, the Moro Islamic Liberation Front (MILF). Yet with the revival of competitive electoral politics and the re-decentralization of law enforcement in the late 1980s and early 1990s, the southern Philippines witnessed the domestication and incorporation of many such Muslim "rebels," some of whom had already been demobilized and co-opted into local government posts since the Tripoli Agreement between the MNLF and the Marcos government in 1976. Local elections in the late 1980s and 1990s saw the elevation of numerous MNLF and MILF commanders and backers to local government positions, revealing and reinforcing the close linkages between the rival armed groups, on the one hand, and local and national electoral politics, on the other. Local Muslim "rebel" commanders became municipal mayors, provincial governors, and congressmen, and thus developed diverse—and divisive—alliances with (Christian) politicians and businessmen in Manila and elsewhere in the country.

> *in the Philippines, a rash of bombings…has unfolded in the midst of considerable setbacks for Islamic causes*

The project of unifying the Muslims of the southern Philippines tended to dissolve in the absorptive webs of the country's highly decentralized democracy. In the context of both formal peace talks and informal political alliances, the MNLF in 1996 agreed to cease armed struggle in exchange for government backing of Nur Misuari's bid for the governorship of the newly created Autonomous Region of Muslim Mindanao (ARMM), even as the avowedly more hard-line MILF continued to exercise influence through elected officials in its stronghold in central Mindanao. The southern Philippines' supposed Muslim separatist "rebels" were in fact largely operating in local political networks and protection rackets and engaging in diverse forms of collaboration with Christian politicians and businessmen. The terms of exchange between these "rebels" in Mindanao and the Sulu Archipelago and their Christian counterparts in Manila accorded substantial powers and prerogatives to MNLF and MILF in these Muslim areas of the Philippines (McKenna 1998).

With the landslide victory of Joseph Estrada in the presidential elections of 1998, however, both the MNLF and the MILF lost their access and influence in Manila to a group of aggressive Catholic politicians with major business interests (logging and mining concessions, coconut plantations) in Muslim areas of Mindanao and the Sulu Archipelago. Egged on by these politicians, and unencumbered by the kinds of electoral alliances with Muslims that had restrained his predecessors, President Estrada declared a "total war" against the MILF in early 2000, launching large-scale military operations that demolished the MILF's camps in Mindanao (Gaerlan and Stankovitch 2000). This move represented a dramatic reversal of the long-standing accommodation and cooperation between Muslim "rebels" and Manila-based politicians in the southern Philippines.

It was in the wake of this dramatic offensive that the first wave of Islamist terrorist activities unfolded in the Philippines in 2000–01. Beginning in March 2000, a series of well-publicized kidnappings took place in the southern Philippines and on the Malaysian resort island of Sipadan, with Filipino Christians, foreign missionaries, and tourists prominently featured among the victims. These kidnappings were attributed to the shadowy Abu Sayyaf (Bearer of the Sword) Group, which had been held responsible for a wave of violence in the early to mid-1990s amidst the Ramos administration's renegotiation of the terms of exchange with the MNLF, but which had faded from public view since the death of its leader in 1998. Yet the violence was not confined to the southern periphery of the Philippine archipelago. In late December 2000, a series of bombs said to have been planted by Islamist terrorists exploded at various locations in Metro Manila, claiming twenty-two lives (Niksch 2002).

Disregarding such apparent retribution, the new administration in Manila persisted with its offensive in the southern Philippines. In 2001, Gloria Macapagal-Arroyo, Estrada's successor as president, backed and bankrolled a close palace advisor in the ARMM gubernatorial elections, a move that spurred the outgoing governor Misuari to launch a desperate MNLF attack on local military outposts in the southern Philippines and then to flee with his forces to neighboring Malaysia. A few years later, with Misuari extradited from Malaysia and imprisoned outside Manila, and with U.S.-backed Philippine government troops occupying former MILF and MNLF strongholds in Maguindanao and Sulu, the struggle for an independent Moro nation in the southern Philippines had clearly run aground. Indeed, in early 2003 U.S. and Philippine troops launched a major offensive in Sulu to root out the remnants of the Abu Sayyaf Group, who were said to have abandoned their strongholds in Basilan and moved to Jolo. Simultaneous operations were launched against the MILF in Mindanao (Lum and Niksch 2006: 13–15; Docena 2007). Later the same year, the MILF agreed to a formal ceasefire with the Philippine government and offered informal cooperation in joint U.S.-Philippine operations to root out Islamist terrorists in the southern Philippines, including Indonesians allegedly affiliated with Jemaah Islamiyah and other such groups (Buendia 2005).

Such was the backdrop to the rash of bombings of 2003–05 in the Philippines, with explosions attributed to the shadowy Abu Sayyaf Group occurring in the southern cities of Davao and General Santos, on a ferry in Manila Bay, and on a bus on a major thoroughfare in Manila (Banlaoi 2006). In previous years, Abu Sayyaf had mostly restricted itself to predatory activities—kidnappings, bank robberies, extortion—within Basilan, the neighboring Zamboanga Peninsula, and other nearby isles in the Sulu Archipelago (Turner 1995; Vitug and Gloria 2000: 192–245). Its activities were confined within a peripheral area of the Philippines, within which it clearly enjoyed close links with local government officials and collusive relations with local law enforcement agencies. For example, Wahab Akbar, provincial governor of Basilan, was not only a former MNLF commander and Islamic preacher, but also one of the founders of the Abu Sayyaf Group. But the violent intrusions of Philippine government forces and U.S. troops in Muslim areas of Mindanao and the Sulu Archipelago and the dramatic defeats and humiliations suffered by the MILF and MNLF since 2000 appear to have spurred at least some armed Islamic groups in the southern Philippines to experiment with more dramatic and deadly terrorist activities much farther afield.

Yet the terrorist bombings of the past few years bear ample evidence of the weakness of the Islamic cause in the southern Philippines rather than its strength. After all, the armed struggle for an independent Moro homeland has ground to a halt, and the limitations of autonomy under the ARMM have been starkly revealed. The armed presence of Philippine government troops and their U.S. backers in the southern Philippines has been greatly increased, giving Manila enhanced leverage vis-à-vis local brokers for Muslim aspirations, interests, and votes. The forced dislocation and deprivation suffered by hundreds of thousands of Muslim Filipinos in the southern Philippines over the past several years of renewed armed conflict may well have heightened Moro resentments against Manila

Abu Sayyaf Group...[also] use[s] violence...to terrorize the putative enemies of Islam...[and] engage in...extortion

and strengthened Muslim identification with co-religionists in some ways (International Displacement Monitoring Centre 2007), but there is little evidence that these developments have generated any greater enthusiasm for avowedly Islamic struggles that have dragged on for so many years with little apparent success. Indeed, even the supposedly extremist Abu Sayyaf Group appears to use violence not only to terrorize the putative enemies of Islam, but also to engage in its long-standing practice of extortion (*Philippine Daily Inquirer* 2004).

The broader context for these Islamic struggles is a predominantly poor, rural, and uneducated Muslim population in the southern Philippines who appear to be largely unreceptive to calls for stricter adherence to Islamic orthodoxy. This is apparent if one considers the only available ethnographic accounts provided by anthropologists who lived and worked in the region in the 1980s and 1990s. In the Maguindanao stronghold of the MILF, for example, Muslims are reported to "rely on magical charms and amulets and appease local spirits. They are Muslims whose religious practice exhibits a good deal of ritual impropriety, who may drink and gamble, neglect their prayers, and perform religious rituals quite at variance with Islamic orthopraxy. They are Muslims who embrace many ingredients of the highly Westernized culture of their Christian neighbors" (McKenna 1998: 283–84). In the Sulu Archipelago, where Abu Sayyaf has made its appearance, local institutions of religious learning are said to have achieved only limited success in promoting an understanding of Islam as an abstract system of belief (Horvatitch 1994). Proponents of Wahhabi or Salafi interpretations of Islam have to contend with local understandings of women ritual specialists and healers as properly Islamic, and with competing sources of external Islamic influence, most notably Ahmadi teachings, which are seen as deviationist by many mainstream Muslims but have been in circulation in the Sulu Archipelago since the 1950s (Horvatitch 1992: 32–63, 113–51). Thus while the threat of further bombing attacks in the Philippines remains real, the notion of an ascendant Islamist threat in the archipelago is hardly credible. Instead, the Philippine government in Manila has considerably reduced the armed strength of the MNLF, MILF, and Abu Sayyaf Group and rendered the struggle for Moro independence a hopeless cause. The small forces mobilized behind the banner of Islam in the southern Philippines are today extremely weak, divided, and on the defensive, with the spate of terrorist bombings in recent years reflecting this weakness, as elsewhere in the region.

> *forces mobilized behind the banner of Islam in the southern Philippines are today extremely weak*

Thailand: Thaksin Shinawatra and Rising Violence in the South

A somewhat similar pattern is evident in Thailand, which has also seen a resurgence of violence in its Muslim south in recent years. As in the Philippines, a small-scale separatist movement in the Islamized southern provinces of the country had lain largely dormant for two decades as the entrenchment of democracy opened up new avenues for southern Thai Muslim politicians to exercise influence in Bangkok's highly fragmented parliament, with the interparty Wahdah faction representing Muslim MPs in Parliament emerging as early as the mid- to late 1980s (Noiwong 2001). The Democrat Party, one of the leading parties throughout the 1990s and a dominant force in the southern provinces, was a crucial vehicle in this regard. Through the Democrats, Muslim politicians won unprecedented access to power and patronage in Bangkok, as most famously exemplified by Surin Pitsuwan, who served as Thailand's foreign minister from 1992 to 2001.[4] The trickle-down effects of this state of affairs made for deepening linkages between local Muslim worthies, small-scale businessmen, and gangsters and Bangkok-based patronage networks (McCargo 2005: 30–33). These networks also included influential elements within the bureaucracy, with former army commander and prime minister Prem Tinsulanond, a close advisor to the king, assuming a prominent role in managing Bangkok's relations with the south. As Duncan McCargo, a leading specialist on Thai politics, has noted:

> Right up until 2001, Prem was often able personally to determine who was selected to serve as provincial governors, senior military commanders, and other key administrative posts in Pattani, Yala, and Narathiwat. This was all part of the deal.
>
> Other elements in the deal included: promoting local Muslims to positions in the bureaucracy, notably as district officers; giving local military commanders carte blanche to "secure" and oversee the Malaysian border (in effect, a license to coax or to extort rents and commissions from those engaged in illegal border trade); providing "development" funds and projects to the subregion, managed by the military, and so permitting the creation of local patronage networks; and cultivating a grassroots network of informers who would tip off the military about actual or potential "separatist" activity. At the same time, local Muslims were encouraged to enter politics, contesting parliamentary seats and gaining ministerial posts under the auspices of the Democrat and later the New Aspiration Party. Administratively, this deal was managed via bodies such as the SBPAC (Southern Border Provinces Administrative Center), under the oversight of the Interior Ministry. (McCargo 2007: 40–41)

With the landslide victory of Thaksin Shinawatra's Thai Rak Thai Party in the January 2001 elections, however, this pattern of incorporation and relative empowerment for local politicians in Thailand's Muslim south was abruptly reversed. Not only did the Thai Rak Thai victory spell defeat for the Democrat Party in particular, but Thaksin's ability to assume the prime ministership without cobbling together a coalition of parties diminished the leverage of all provincial politicians vis-à-vis Bangkok. After a decade of fragmented parliamentary politics in Thailand, in which successive cabinets incorporated provincial *chao pho* (godfathers) into ruling coalitions, the sudden (re)centralization of power in the hands of a figure reminiscent of Italy's Silvio Berlusconi (or Russia's Vladimir Putin) had important local consequences in the Muslim southern provinces of Thailand, in terms of the awarding of construction contracts, the regulation of local businesses, and the enforcement of laws on smuggling, gambling, and narcotics trafficking. Accompanying—and enforcing—Thaksin's recentralizing drive, moreover, was a restrengthening of the police and the military establishment over provincial politicians, businessmen, and gangsters, which had a particular relevance for provinces with significant illegal economies and security problems, such as the Muslim provinces of southern Thailand. In the aftermath of the September 11, 2001 attacks on New York City and Washington, D.C., moreover, the advantages of reasserting control over the "lawless" Muslim south were no longer solely domestic, given the rewards offered by the Bush administration for vigilance and cooperation in the Global War on Terrorism (Phongpaichit and Baker 2004; McCargo and Pathmanand 2004).

Within a few short years, this reassertion of Bangkok's control over the Muslim provinces of southern Thailand had led to the outbreak of violence. Upon his election, Thaksin initiated an aggressive campaign to dismantle the Democrat Party's patronage networks in the south, with policy changes most publicly visible in the realm of internal security and law enforcement. Important bodies for the coordination of policing and intelligence gathering like the SBPAC and the joint army-police-civilian unit known as CMP-43 were abolished, and command over local army and police units was recentralized in the hands of officers in Bangkok closely allied with Thaksin. The trickle-down effects of these changes were undoubtedly significant for local politicians, civilian bureaucrats and policemen, businessmen, smugglers, and other gangsters in the Muslim provinces of southern Thailand, as previous arrangements for the division of the spoils of power and understandings about the enforcement of the law were abruptly cancelled after nearly a decade of continuity (Croissant 2001: 31–35; International Crisis Group 2005b: 33–36).

The resulting violence was not long in coming. Small-scale attacks on government security forces by armed Muslim groups in the south began to rise in 2002 and 2003. A series of large-scale incidents followed in 2004: a major assault on an army depot where several hundred arms were seized in January, a set of coordinated attacks on almost a dozen government security posts in April, and a mass protest outside a police station in October. In all of these incidents, Thai security forces killed large numbers of Muslims, including dozens massacred in a major mosque and dozens more asphyxiated in a truck while in transit to a detention center. Martial law was declared in early 2004, and a special emergency decree was promulgated in mid-2005, but the violence steadily continued with shootings and bombings, and there were estimated to be more than one thousand casualties by early 2006 (Amnesty International 2006a).

A few features of the violence are worthy of note. First of all, most of those killed were Muslims, and even the large-scale attacks on government security posts left few Thai military or police casualties, in contrast to the many dozens of alleged Muslim attackers left dead after these incidents (Human Rights Watch 2007). More important, perhaps, was the continuing lack of evidence about the presence or activity of any real organization promoting armed mobilization among Muslims—whether *qua* Muslims or otherwise—in southern Thailand (*International Herald Tribune* 2004c; *Asia Times* 2004). As one observer noted, "not a single Malay-Muslim has yet been convicted of actual violence and not a single militant organization has yet been exposed on the basis of verifiable information" (Liow 2006b: 91). At the same time, ethnographic accounts of Islam in the rural hamlets of southern Thailand offered little evidence of increasing receptivity toward or adherence to forms of orthodoxy associated with the Salafi currents linked to transnational *jihadi* networks (Horstmann 2002; Janchitfah 2004). In other words, it remained very unclear whether there was "much of a there there" in the Muslim provinces of southern Thailand, and how much of the "there" there was in fact of a plausibly Islamist nature.

The forced ouster of Thaksin by a military coup in September 2006 raised hopes that the trend toward violence in the south could be reversed and that the pre-2001 status quo could be reestablished. Indeed, the éminence grise said to be behind the coup—the king's close advisor Prem Tinsulanond—had been the architect of Bangkok's successful reintegration of the southern Muslim provinces in the 1980s and 1990s, and the army general who led the coup had extensive experience in the south and was known to have bitterly disagreed with Thaksin over government policy in the region. The newly appointed prime minister issued a public apology to Muslims in southern Thailand, and the new government promised to reestablish a version of the SBPAC and to begin negotiations with leaders of the insurgency (*International Herald Tribune* 2006b).

By early 2007, however, it had become clear that the short-term consequences of the coup were less than salutary for the southern provinces of Thailand. Violent incidents increased in frequency and intensity in the last three months of 2006, with this rise in violence "accompanied by a pattern of provocative attacks on teachers, monks and other civilians, often involving burning or mutilation of corpses" (International Crisis Group 2007: 8). Mid-February 2007 witnessed a set of coordinated bombings and arson attacks across southern Thailand, as observers noted a broader pattern of recruitment and mobilization in many Muslim villages in the region (Ibid.: 9–12). Conciliatory gestures and personnel turnover aside, the new government appears to have done little to reverse the recentralization instituted by Thaksin, with the terms of exchange decidedly weighted in favor of army generals in Bangkok at the expense of local Muslim power brokers in the southern provinces of the country. With criticism of the new government's supposedly conciliatory approach rising in Bangkok, there are signs of a new strategy of mobilizing local civilian militias—along the lines of the mobilization of the anti-communist Village Scouts in the 1970s—against the insurgents in the south (*International Herald Tribune* 2007; Bowie 1997). But only with the resumption of competitive electoral politics will a return to the peaceful accommodation of the 1990s be possible in southern Thailand.

Conclusion: Much Ado about Nothing?

In conclusion, the preceding pages have cast considerable doubt on the conventional alarmist picture of ascendant, aggressive Islamist forces threatening Southeast Asia with terrorist violence and a broader campaign of religious extremism, intolerance, and expanding influence. The tendency toward selection bias and sensationalism in the coverage of Islamist activity and influence in the region has led to the exaggeration of the strength of Islamist forces and to a misleading picture of Islamist expansion. Against this tendency, the preceding account of Islamist forces and fortunes in

Southeast Asia has stressed not only the weakness of Islamist movements and parties, but also the overall *decline* in Islamist authority and influence over the past several years. To be sure, small groups of Islamist terrorists may still be capable of another single annual bombing of a "soft" Western target in Indonesia, as they did in 2002. Further bombings are also still likely in the Philippines,

not much more collective violence should be anticipated by Southeast Asia's nearly 250 million Muslims

and there is ample reason to expect more attacks in southern Thailand. However, not much more collective violence should be anticipated by Southeast Asia's nearly 250 million Muslims.

As for broader Islamist influence in the region, the PKS may continue to expand its share of the national and local vote in Indonesia, the PAS will survive if not prosper in Malaysia, and the MILF in the southern Philippines will do the same. Perhaps some kind of identifiably Islamic organization will even emerge to champion the cause of the beleaguered Muslim minority in the southern provinces of Thailand. The Islamist élan so evident in Indonesia and Malaysia in 1998–99, however, is gone, as is the confidence and credibility enjoyed by brokers for the Muslim vote in the southern provinces of the Philippines and Thailand from the mid-1980s through the late 1990s. Muslim political consciousness and religiosity may be strong in Southeast Asia, but established Islamic authority structures in the region have weakened, not unlike

The Islamist élan so evident in Indonesia and Malaysia in 1998–99…is gone

the Catholic Church in many parts of the Philippines and the Theravada Buddhist *sangha* in Thailand. The hegemony of the old ecclesiastical establishments has eroded; the position of new claimants to religious power remains fragile and in flux. In this era of globalization, democratization, and what Olivier Roy calls "deterritorialization," new forms of religious practice, communication, and mediation have begun to undermine the established structures of religious authority, giving rise to a more fragmented and fluctuating pattern of religious life, for Muslims as well as for practitioners of other faiths in Southeast Asia. The notion of a coherent, unified Islamist threat, then, is hardly credible.

In addition to providing an alternative *descriptive* account, this study has also suggested something equally contrarian with regard to the *explanation* for recent trends, as well as the *implications* for Southeast Asia and for policy makers concerned about the region. The turn toward terrorist violence by small numbers of Islamist militants in Southeast Asia over the past several years must be understood as a symptom of and reaction to the decline, domestication, and disentanglement from state power of Islamist forces in the region. The shift to violence, moreover, came in the face of considerable aggression and provocation by non-Muslim and anti-Islamist forces in the region, aided and encouraged by the United States and its allies in the prosecution of the Global War on Terrorism. Likewise, the pattern of apparent Islamist assertiveness and expanding Islamic regulatory efforts in Malaysia and Indonesia is best understood in the context of the threats posed to established religious hierarchies, identities, and boundaries. These threats stemmed from economic growth, urbanization, and expanding access to non-Muslim sources of education, information, and entertainment, as well as from the pressures of electoral competition, both national and local, in these two countries.

For those concerned about Southeast Asia, a set of implications follows from this alternative descriptive and explanatory account of the Islamist threat in the region. For example, if the threat of Islamist terrorism has been exaggerated and manipulated by non-Muslim and anti-Islamist governments in Southeast Asia, then much more should be done to address the self-evident side effects of the enlistment of the region's security forces in the Global War on Terrorism.

> *much more should be done to address the…effects of the enlistment of the region's security forces in the Global War on Terrorism*

In Indonesia, the Philippines, and Thailand, the threat of Islamist violence has allowed police, military, and intelligence services to regain some of the influence in politics, international funding and assistance, and insulation from public scrutiny that they lost during the preceding years of democratization and demilitarization.

The pursuit of the Global War on Terrorism in Southeast Asia has coincided with rising evidence of criminal—and homicidal—activity by Indonesian intelligence (BIN), a campaign of intimidation and assassination against left-wing activists in the Philippines, and a parallel pattern of human rights abuses by the army and the police in Thaksin's Thailand (Amnesty International 2006b). Moreover, in all three countries, and in Malaysia with its application of the Internal Security Act after 1999, the use of the security forces by civilian leaders to pursue partisan political ends has been greatly facilitated

> *the use of the security forces...to pursue partisan political ends has been greatly facilitated by the cover of counterterrorist... campaigns*

by the cover of counterterrorist and counterinsurgency campaigns. The effective promotion of democratization, the rule of law, and good governance in Southeast Asia requires a closer, more critical, and more constructive assessment of the uses and abuses of the Islamist threat in the region.

A principled commitment to the promotion of democratization in Southeast Asia might lead to a reconsideration of the very nature of the so-called Islamist threat in the region by posing the obvious question: a threat to *whom*, a threat to *what?* In large measure, the answer to this question is clear: a threat to the prevailing pattern of oligarchy and machine politics in Southeast Asia, in which non-Islamists and non-Muslims have long been the dominant force. Without the PKS, Indonesia would certainly be less democratic; without PAS, Malaysia would obviously be even more undemocratic. If Islamic education and associational life were stronger, civil society would undoubtedly be more vibrant in the southern Muslim provinces of the Philippines and Thailand, and thus more capable of constraining local abuses of state power. As a basis for mobilizing voters, for aggregating interests, and for exercising state power, Islam certainly represents an important alternative or complement to the predominant forms of money politics, clientelism, cronyism, and corruption. Thus, if democratization, good governance, and the rule of law constitute a worthy cause in Southeast Asia, then the Islamist threat in the region should not be allowed to serve as an excuse for compromise, qualification, or delay, and should instead be enlisted as an important asset in the service of the cause.

Endnotes

1. The ICG's reports on Thailand (e.g. International Crisis Group 2005b: 20) are a noteworthy exception to this rule, standing in sharp contrast to their coverage of Indonesia and the Philippines.
2. For a more even-handed approach along these lines with reference to another region in the Muslim world, see De Waal 2004.
3. Of the 153 members of the PDI-P elected to the People's Representative Assembly (Dewan Perwakilan Rakyat or DPR) in 1999, only 96 (63 percent) were registered as Muslims, with at least 36 Protestants (23 percent), 12 Catholics, and 7 Hindus among the remaining MPs. See *Wajah Dewan* (2000: 3–155).
4. He also wrote a Harvard doctoral dissertation on Islam and separatism in southern Thailand (Pitsuwan 1982).

Bibliography

Abinales, Patricio N. 2000. *Making Mindanao: Cotabato and Davao in the Formation of the Philippine Nation-State.* Quezon City: Ateneo de Manila University Press.

Abuza, Zachary. 2002. "Tentacles of Terror: Al Qaeda's Southeast Asian Network." *Contemporary Southeast Asia* 24(3): 427–65.

———. 2003. *Militant Islam in Southeast Asia: Crucible of Terror.* Boulder, CO: Lynne Rienner.

———. 2004. *Muslims, Politics, and Violence in Indonesia: An Emerging Jihadist-Islamist Nexus?* Seattle: National Bureau of Asian Research, September.

———. 2005. "The Moro Islamic Liberation Front at 20: State of the Revolution." *Studies in Conflict and Terrorism* 28: 453–79.

———. 2006. *Balik-Terrorism: The Return of the Abu Sayyaf.* Carlisle, PA: Strategic War Studies Institute, U.S. Army War College, September.

———. 2007. *Political Islam and Violence in Indonesia.* London: Routledge.

Agence France Presse. 2006. "Malaysia Puts Islamic Bill on Hold after Furore." January 12.

Al Chaidar. 2000. *Lampung Bersimbah Darah: Menelusuri Kejahatan "Negara Intelijen" Orde Baru Dalam Peristiwa Jama'ah Warsidi.* Jakarta: Madani Press.

Amnesty International. 2006a. "Thailand: Locals Trapped by Escalating Violence in the South." January 4.

———. 2006b. *Philippines: Political Killings, Human Rights and the Peace Process.* London: Amnesty International, August.

Anderson, Benedict R. O'G. 1972. *Java in a Time of Revolution: Occupation and Resistance, 1944–1946.* Ithaca, NY: Cornell University Press.

Asia Times. 2004. "Thailand's Southern Blame Game." December 18.

———. 2006a. "Indonesian Dancer, Clerics Go Toe-to-Toe." June 21.

———. 2006b. "Malaysian Minorities Wary of Islamist Overtures." June 15.

Assegaff, Farha Abdul Kadir. 1995. "Peran Perempuan Islam (Penelitian di Pondok

Pesantren Al Mukmin, Sukoharjo, Jawa Tengah)." Tesis S-2, Program Studi Sosiologi, Fakultas Ilmu Sosial, Gadjah Mada University.

Awwas, Irfan S. 2000. *Trauma Lampung Berdarah: Di Balik Manuver Hendro Priyono.* Yogyakarta: Wihdah Press.

Banlaoi, Rommel C. 2006. "The Abu Sayyaf Group: Threat of Maritime Piracy and Terrorism." In Lehr, Peter, ed. 2006. *Violence at Sea: Piracy in the Age of Global Terrorism.* London: Routledge.

———. 2007. "The Abu Sayyaf Group: From Mere Banditry to Genuine Terrorism." In *Southeast Asian Affairs 2006.* 2007. Singapore: Institute of Southeast Asian Studies: 247–62.

Bennett, Linda Rae. 2005. *Women, Islam and Modernity: Single Women, Sexuality and Reproductive Health in Contemporary Indonesia.* London: RoutledgeCurzon.

Blackburn, Susan. 2001. "Women and the Nation," *Inside Indonesia*, April–June.

Boellstorff, Tom. 2004. "The Emergence of Political Homophobia in Indonesia: Masculinity and National Belonging." *Ethnos* 69(4): 465–86.

———. 2005a. "Between Religion and Desire: Being Muslim and *Gay* in Indonesia." *American Anthropologist* 107(4): 575–85.

———. 2005b. *The Gay Archipelago: Sexuality and Nation in Indonesia.* Princeton, NJ: Princeton University Press.

Bowen, John R. 2003. *Islam, Law and Equality in Indonesia: An Anthropology of Public Reasoning.* Cambridge: Cambridge University Press.

Bowie, Katherine A. 1997. *Rituals of National Loyalty: An Anthropology of the State and the Village Scout Movement in Thailand.* New York: Columbia University Press.

Brenner, Suzanne. 1996. "Reconstructing Self and Society: Javanese Muslim Women and 'The Veil'." *American Ethnologist* 23(4): 673–97.

———. 2005. "Islam and Gender Politics in Late New Order Indonesia." In Wilford, Andrew C., and George, Kenneth M., eds. 2005. *Spirited Politics: Religion and Public Life in Contemporary Southeast Asia.* Ithaca, NY: Cornell University Southeast Asia Program.

Buendia, Rizal G. 2005. "The GRP-MILF Peace Talks: Quo Vadis?" In *Southeast Asian Affairs 2004.* Singapore: Institute of Southeast Asian Affairs.

Burnham, Gracia. 2003. *In the Presence of My Enemies.* Wheaton, IL: Tyndal House Publishers.

Cahyono, Heru. 1992. *Peranan Ulama Dalam Golkar, 1971–1980: Dari Pemilu Sampai Malari.* Jakarta: Pustaka Sinar Harapan.

———. 1998. *Pangkopkamtib Jenderal Soemitro dan Peristiwa 15 Januari '74.* Jakarta: Pustaka Sinar Harapan.

Clark, Janine A. 2006. "The Conditions of Islamist Moderation: Unpacking Cross-Ideological Cooperation in Jordan." *International Journal of Middle East Studies* 38(4): 539–60.

Collins, Elizabeth Fuller. 2004. "Islam and the Habits of Democracy: Islamic Organizations in Post–New Order South Sumatra." *Indonesia* 78: 93–120.

Conboy, Ken. 2004. *Intel: Inside Indonesia's Intelligence Service.* Jakarta: Equinox.

Croissant, Aurel. 2005. "Unrest in South Thailand: Contours, Causes, and Consequences Since 2001." *Contemporary Southeast Asia* 27(1): 21–43.

Damanik, Ali Said. 2000. *Fenomena Partai Keadilan: Transformasi 20 Tahun Gerakan Tarbiyah di Indonesia.* Jakarta: Teraju.

Davidson, Jamie S., and David Henley, eds. 2007. *The Revival of Tradition in Indonesian Politics*. London: Routledge.

Davis, Michael. 2002. "Laskar Jihad and the Political Position of Conservative Islam in Indonesia." *Contemporary Southeast Asia* 24(1): 12–32.

De Waal, Alex, ed. 2004. *Islamism and Its Enemies in the Horn of Africa*. London: C. Hurst.

Docena, Herbert. 2007. *Unconventional Warfare: Are US Special Forces engaged in an 'offensive war' in the Philippines?* Quezon City: Focus on the Global South, January.

Far Eastern Economic Review. 2001. "Of Missiles and Terrorism." November 8.

Faruqi, Shad Saleem. 2005. "The Malaysian Constitution, The Islamic State and *Hudud* Laws." In Nathan, K. S., and Mohammad Hashim Kamali, eds. 2005. *Islam in Southeast Asia: Political, Social and Strategic Challenges in the 21ˢᵗ Century*. Singapore: Institute of Southeast Asian Studies.

Feillard, Andreé. 1995. *Islam et armée dans l'Indonésie contemporaine*. Paris: L'Harmattan.

Freedman, Maurice. 1960. "The Growth of a Plural Society in Malaya." *Pacific Affairs* 33(2): 158–68.

Furkon, Aay Muhamad. 2004. *Partai Keadilan Sejahtera: Ideologi dan Praksis Politik Kaum Muda Muslim Indonesia Kontemporer*. Jakarta: Teraju.

Gaerlan, Kristina, and Mara Stankovitch, eds. 2000. *Rebels, Warlords and Ulama: A Reader on Muslim Separatism and the War in the Southern Philippines*. Quezon City: Institute for Popular Democracy.

Gatra. 2006a. "Gelora Syariah Mengepung Kota." May 6.

———. 2006b. "Menguji Niat Baik Perda." May 6.

———. 2006c. "Aneka Ragam Laskar Jalanan." June 15.

Gershman, John. 2002. "Is Southeast Asia the Second Front?" *Foreign Affairs* 81(4): 20–74.

Gomez, Edmund Terence. 1999. *Chinese Business in Malaysia: Accumulation, Accommodation and Resistance* Richmond: Curzon.

Gutierrez, Eric, and Saturnino Borras Jr. 2004. *The Moro Conflict: Landlessness and Misdirected State Policies*. Policy Studies 8. Washington, D.C.: East-West Center Washington.

Hafez, Muhammed M. 2003. *Why Muslims Rebel: Repression and Resistance in the Islamic World*. Boulder, CO: Lynne Rienner.

Hamayotsu, Kikue. 2005. "Demobilizing Islam: Institutionalized Religion and the Politics of Co-optation in Malaysia." Ph.D. dissertation, Australian National University.

Hasan, Noorhaidi. 2006. *Laskar Jihad: Islam, Militancy, and the Quest for Identity in Post–New Order Indonesia*. Ithaca, NY: Cornell University Southeast Asia Program.

Hefner, Robert W. 1993. "Islam, State, and Civil Society: ICMI and the Struggle for the Indonesian Middle Class." *Indonesia* 56: 1–35.

Henderson, J. Vernon, and Ari Kuncoro. 2006. *Sick of Local Government Corruption? Vote Islamic*. Cambridge, MA: National Bureau of Economic Research, March.

Hirschman, Charles. 1986. "The Making of Race in Colonial Malaya: Political Economy and Racial Ideology." *Sociological Forum* 1(2): 330–61.

Hooker, M. B. 2003. *Indonesian: Islam: Social Change through Contemporary Fatāwā*. Honolulu: University of Hawai'i Press.

Horikoshi, Hiroko. 1975. "The Dar Ul-Islam Movement in West Java (1948–62): An Experience in the Historical Process." *Indonesia* 20: 59–86.

Horstmann, Alexander. 2002. *Class, Culture and Space: The Construction and Shaping of Communal Space in Southern Thailand.* Bielefeld, Germany: Transcript Publishers.

Horvatitch, Patricia. 1992. "Mosques and Misunderstandings: Muslim Discourses in Tawi-Tawi, Philippines." Ph.D. dissertation, Stanford University.

———. 1994. "Ways of Knowing Islam." *American Ethnologist* 21(4): 811–26.

Hosen, Nadirsyah. 2005. "Religion and the Indonesian Constitution: A Recent Debate." *Journal of Southeast Asian Studies* 36(3): 419–40.

Howell, Julia Day. 2001. "Sufism and the Indonesian Islamic Revival." *Journal of Asian Studies* 60(3): 701–29.

———. 2005. "Muslims, the New Age and Marginal Religions in Indonesia: Changing Meanings of Religious Pluralism." *Social Compass* 52(4): 473–93.

Human Rights Watch. 2004. *In the Name of Security: Counterterrorism and Human Rights Abuses under Malaysia's Internal Security Act.* New York: Human Rights Watch.

———. 2007. *"It Was Like Suddenly My Son No Longer Existed": Enforced Disappearances in Thailand's Southern Border Provinces.* New York: Human Rights Watch, March.

Ichwan, Moch. Nur. 2005. "'Ulamā', State and Politics: Majelis Ulama Indonesia after Suharto." *Islamic Law and Society* 12(1): 45–72.

Ileto, Reynaldo S. 1971. *Magindanao 1860–1888: The Career of Datu Uto of Buayan.* Ithaca, NY: Cornell University Southeast Asia Program.

International Crisis Group (ICG). 2002a. *Al-Qaeda in Southeast Asia: The Case of the "Ngruki Network" in Indonesia.* Jakarta and Brussels: International Crisis Group, August.

———. 2002b. *Indonesia Backgrounder: How the Jemaah Islamiyah Terrorist Network Operates.* Jakarta and Brussels: International Crisis Group, December.

———. 2003. *Jemaah Islamiyah in South East Asia: Damaged but Still Dangerous.* Jakarta and Brussels: International Crisis Group, August.

———. 2004a. *Indonesia Backgrounder: Jihad in Central Sulawesi.* Jakarta and Brussels: International Crisis Group, February.

———. 2004b. *Southern Philippines Backgrounder: Terrorism and the Peace Process.* Singapore and Brussels: International Crisis Group, July.

———. 2004c. *Southern Philippines Backgrounder: Terrorism and the Peace Process.* Jakarta and Brussels: International Crisis Group, July.

———. 2004d. *Indonesia Backgrounder: Why Salafism and Terrorism Mostly Don't Mix.* Singapore and Brussels: International Crisis Group, September.

———. 2005a. *Recycling Militants in Indonesia: Darul Islam and the Australian Embassy Bombing.* Singapore and Brussels: International Crisis Group, February.

———. 2005b. *Southern Thailand: Insurgency, Not Jihad.* Singapore and Brussels: International Crisis Group, May.

———. 2005c. *Weakening Indonesia's Mujahidin Networks: Lessons from Maluku and Poso.* Jakarta and Brussels: International Crisis Group, October.

———. 2005d. *Philippines Terrorism: The Role of Militant Islamic Converts.* Jakarta and Brussels: International Crisis Group, December.

———. 2006a. *Terrorism in Indonesia: Noordin's Networks.* Jakarta and Brussels: International Crisis Group, May.

———. 2006b. *Islamic Law and Criminal Justice in Aceh.* Jakarta and Brussels:
International Crisis Group, July.

———. 2007. *Southern Thailand: The Impact of the Coup.* Jakarta and Brussels:
International Crisis Group, March.

International Displacement Monitoring Centre. 2007. *Philippines: More Attention Needed
on Protection of IDPs.* Geneva: Internal Displacement Monitoring Centre,
Norwegian Refugee Council, March.

International Herald Tribune. 2004a. "Indonesian Islamist Party is Quietly Gaining
Ground." April 8.

———. 2004b. "An Islamic Leader Rises in Indonesian Politics." October 21.

———. 2004c. "Thailand: Behind the Muslim 'insurgency'." December 17.

———. 2005a. "Malaysians Sour on Muslim Vigilantes." March 26–27.

———. 2005b. "Islamic Rule Faces a Test in Malaysia." December 6.

———. 2006a "Malaysia's Big Sister Shakes up Islamic Rule." February 17.

———. 2006b. "A Lighter Touch Eases Southern Thai's Mood." October 18.

———. 2006c. "Malaysia's Anwar: Government Stifling Non-Muslims' Rights."
December 16.

———. 2007. "Use of Militias Is Rising in Southern Thailand." March 20.

Jakarta Post. 2005a. "MUI to Formulate Edicts against 'Liberal Thoughts'." July 27.

———. 2005b. "Police Investigate Church Closures, Vow to Take Action." September 13.

Janchitfah, Supara. 2004. *Violence in the Mist: Reporting on the Presence of Pain in
Southern Thailand.* Bangkok: Korbai Publishing Project.

Jenkins, David. 1984. *Suharto and His Generals: Indonesian Military Politics, 1975–1983.*
Ithaca, NY: Cornell Modern Indonesia Project.

Jesudason, James V. 1990. *Ethnicity and the Economy: The State, Chinese, Business, and
Multinationals in Malaysia.* Singapore: Oxford University Press.

Jones, Gavin W. 1976. "Religion and Education in Indonesia." *Indonesia* 22: 19–56.

Juhannis, Hamdan. 2006. "The Struggle for Formalist Islam in South Sulawesi: From
Darul Islam (DI) to Komite Persiapan Penegakan Syariat Islam." Ph.D. dissertation,
Australian National University.

Kalyvas, Stathis. 1996. *Religious Mobilization and Party Formation: Confessional Parties
and the Christian Democratic Phenomenon.* Ithaca, NY: Cornell University Press.

Kahin, George McT. 1952. *Nationalism and Revolution in Indonesia.* Ithaca, NY: Cornell
University Press.

Karpat, Kemal H. 2001. *The Politicization of Islam: Reconstructing Identity, State, Faith,
and Community in the Late Ottoman State.* Oxford: Oxford University Press.

Kepel, Gilles. 2000. *Jihad: The Trail of Political Islam.* Cambridge, MA: Harvard
University Press.

Kompas. 2005. "Fatwa MUI Memicu Kontroversi; Ma'ruf Amin: MUI Siap
Menanggapi." July 30.

Laffan, Michael Francis. 2002. *Islamic Nationhood and Colonial Indonesia: The Umma
below the Winds.* London: RoutledgeCurzon.

Langhor, Vickie. 2001. "Of Islamists and Ballot Boxes: Rethinking the Relationship
between Islamists and Electoral Politics." *International Journal of Middle East Studies*
33(4): 591–610.

Liddle, R. William. 1996. "The Islamic Turn in Indonesia: A Political Explanation."
Journal of Asian Studies 55(3): 613–34.

Linrung, Tamsil. 2003. *ManilaGate: Kontroversi Penangkapan Tamsil Linrung*. Jakarta: Merah Putih.

Liow, Joseph Chinyong. 2004a. "Exigency or Expediency? Contextualising Political Islam and the PAS Challenge in Malaysian Politics." *Third World Quarterly* 25(2): 359–72.

———. 2004b. "Political Islam in Malaysia: Problematising Discourse and Practice in the UMNO-PAS 'Islamisation Race'." *Commonwealth and Comparative Politics* 42(4): 184–205.

———. 2005. "The Politics behind Malaysia's Eleventh General Election." *Asian Survey* 45(6): 907–30.

———. 2006a. "Prospects for Reform in PAS." *IDSS Commentaries*, August 28.

———. 2006b. "International Jihad and Muslim Radicalism in Thailand? Toward an Alternative Interpretation." *Asia Policy* 2: 91.

Lum, Thomas, and Larry A. Niksch. 2006. *The Republic of the Philippines: Background and U.S. Relations*. Report RL 33233. Washington, D.C.: Congressional Research Service Report of the Library of Congress, January 10.

Martinez, Patricia A. 2001. "The Islamic State or the State of Islam in Malaysia." *Contemporary Southeast Asia* 23(3): 474–503.

McCargo, Duncan. 2005. "Southern Thai Politics: A Preliminary Overview." In Sugunnasil, Wattana, ed. 2005. *Dynamic Diversity in Southern Thailand*. Chiang Mai: Silkworm Books.

———. 2007. "Thaksin and the Resurgence of Violence in the Thai South." In McCargo, Duncan, ed. 2007. *Rethinking Thailand's Southern Violence*. Singapore: National University of Singapore Press.

McCargo, Duncan, and Ukrist Pathmanand. 2004. *The Thaksinization of Thailand*. Copenhagen: Nordic Institute of Asian Studies.

McKenna, Thomas. 1998. *Muslim Rulers and Rebels: Everyday Politics and Armed Separatism in the Southern Philippines*. Berkeley: University of California Press.

McVey, Ruth. 1989. "Identity and Rebellion Among Southern Thai Muslims." In Forbes, Andrew D. W., ed. 1989. *The Muslims of Thailand: Volume 2: Politics of the Malay-Speaking South*. Gaya, India: Centre for South East Asian Studies.

Mecham, R. Quinn. 2004. "From the Ashes of Virtue, a Promise of Light: The Transformation of Political Islam in Turkey." *Third World Quarterly* 25(2): 339–58.

Mohamed, Zabidi. 2003. *Rahsia dalam Rahsia Maunah: Kebenaran yang Sebenar*. Kuala Lumpur: Zabidi Publication.

Moten, Abdul Rashid, and Tunku Mohar Mokhtar. 2006. "The 2004 General Elections in Malaysia: A Mandate to Rule." *Asian Survey* 46(2): 319–40.

Nasr, Seyyed Vali Reza. 2001. *Islamic Leviathan: Islam and the Making of State Power*. Oxford: Oxford University Press.

———. 2005. "The Rise of 'Muslim Democracy'." *Journal of Democracy* 16(2): 13–27.

Nathan, K. S. 2007. "Malaysia: The Challenge of Money Politics and Religious Activism." In *Southeast Asian Affairs 2006*. Singapore: Institute of Southeast Asian Studies.

The Nation (Bangkok). 2005. "Indonesian Democracy's Enemy Within." December 5.

New Straits Times. 2005a. "Call to Act against Policing of Morality." March 23.

———. 2005b. "Police Must Approve Raids by Religious Department." March 25.

———. 2005c. "State Morality Squad Disbanded." March 26.

———. 2005d. "Caucus against Moral Policing." April 5.

New York Times. 2006a. "Women Caught in a More Radical Indonesia." June 28.

————. 2006b. "Playboy Indonesia: Modest Flesh Meets Muslim Faith." July 24.

Niksch, Larry. 2002. *Abu Sayyaf: Target of Philippine-U.S. Anti-Terrorism Cooperation.* Report RL 31265. Washington, D.C.: Congressional Research Service Report of the Library of Congress, January 25.

Noiwong, Ornanong. 2001. "Political Integration Policies and Strategies of the Thai Government Towards the Malay-Muslims of Southernmost Thailand (1973–2000)." Ph.D. dissertation, Northern Illinois University at De Kalb.

Noor, Farish. 2003. "Blood, Sweat and *Jihad*: The Radicalization of the Political Discourse of the Pan-Malaysian Islamic Party (PAS) from 1982 Onwards." *Contemporary Southeast Asia* 25(2): 200–232.

Noor, Farish A. 2004. *Islam Embedded: The Historical Development of the Pan-Malaysian Islamic Party PAS (1951–2003): Volume 2.* Kuala Lumpur: Malaysian Sociological Research Institute.

Oetomo, Dédé. 2001. "Gay Men in the Reformasi Era: Homophobic Violence Could Be a By-product of the New Openness." *Inside Indonesia*, April–June.

Peletz, Michael G. 1993. "Sacred Texts and Dangerous Words: The Politics of Law and Cultural Rationalization in Malaysia." *Comparative Studies in Society and History* 35(1): 66–109.

————. 2002. *Islamic Modern: Religious Courts and Cultural Politics in Malaysia.* Princeton, NJ: Princeton University Press.

Pemberton, John. 1994. *On the Subject of "Java."* Ithaca, NY: Cornell University Press.

Philippine Daily Inquirer. 2004. "We Bombed Ferry, Claims Abu Sayyaf." February 29.

Phongpaichit, Pasuk, and Chris Baker. 2004. *Thaksin: The Business of Politics in Thailand.* Copenhagen: Nordic Institute of Asian Studies.

Pikiran Rakyat. 2005. "Usulkan 'Reshuffle' Tim Ekonomi, PKS Tetap Loyal kepada Pemerintah." November 28.

Pitsuwan, Surin. 1982. "Islam and Malay Nationalism: A Case Study of the Malay-Muslims of Southern Thailand." Ph.D. dissertation, Harvard University.

Qodir, Zuly. 2003. *Ada Apa Dengan Pondok Pesantren Ngruki.* Bantul, Indonesia: Pondok Edukasi.

Robison, Richard R., and Vedi R. Hadiz. 2004. *Reorganising Power in Indonesia: The Politics of Oligarchy in an Age of Markets.* London: RoutledgeCurzon.

Roff, William R. 1967. *The Origins of Malay Nationalism.* New Haven, CT: Yale University Press.

Roosa, John. 2006. *Pretext for Mass Murder: The September 30th Movement and Suharto's Coup D'État in Indonesia.* Madison: University of Wisconsin Press.

Roy, Olivier. 1995. *The Failure of Political Islam.* Cambridge, MA: Harvard University Press.

————. 2004. *Globalised Islam: The Search for a New Ummah.* London: Hurst.

Rush, James R. 1990. *Opium to Java: Revenue Farming and Chinese Enterprise in Colonial Indonesia, 1860–1910.* Ithaca, NY: Cornell University Press.

Scott, William Henry. 1991. *Slavery in the Spanish Philippines.* Manila: De La Salle University Press.

Schwedler, Jillian. 2006. *Faith in Moderation: Islamist Parties in Jordan and Yemen.* Cambridge: Cambridge University Press.

Searle, Peter. 1999. *The Riddle of Malaysian Capitalism: Rent-seekers or Real Capitalists?* Honolulu: University of Hawai'i Press.

Sen, Krishna. 2005. "Film Revolution? Women Are Now on Both Sides of the Camera." *Inside Indonesia,* July–September.

Sidel, John T. 2006. *Riots, Pogroms, Jihad: Religious Violence in Indonesia.* Ithaca, NY: Cornell University Press.

Sinar Indonesia Baru. 2005. "Pengurus PGI Temui Presiden SBY Minta Usut Tuntas Penutupan Paksa Gereja." August 25.

Singapore Ministry of Home Affairs. 2003. *White Paper: The Jemaah Islamiyah Arrests and the Threat of Terrorism.* Singapore: Ministry of Home Affairs, January 7.

Slater, Dan. 2004. "Indonesia's Accountability Trap: Party Cartels and Presidential Power after Democratic Transition." *Indonesia* 78: 61–92.

Smith-Hefner, Nancy J. 2005. "The New Muslim Romance: Changing Patterns of Courtship and Marriage among Educated Javanese Youth." *Journal of Southeast Asian Studies* 36(3): 441–59.

Soebardi, S. 1983. "Kartosuwiryo and the Darul Islam Rebellion in Indonesia." *Journal of Southeast Asian Studies* 14(1): 109–33.

Soepriyadi, Es. 2003. *Ngruki dan Jaringan Terorisme: Melacak Jejak Abu Bakar Ba'asyir dan Jaringannya dari Ngruki sampai Bom Bali.* Jakarta: Al-Mawardi Prima.

The Star (Penang, Malaysia). 2005. "PAS No. 2 Feeling the Heat." March 20.

Starrett, Gregory. 1998. *Putting Islam to Work: Education, Politics, and Religious Transformation in Egypt.* Berkeley: University of California Press.

Suara Hidayatullah. 2000. "KH Shiddiq Amien, Ketua Umum Persis: Kemusyrikan Dibiarkan, Syariat Malah Ditolak." October.

Suara Rakyat Malaysia (SUARAM). 2006. *Malaysia Human Rights Report 2005: Civil and Political Rights.* Petaling Jaya: Suara Rakyat Malaysia.

Suehiro, Akira. 1992. "Capitalist Development in Postwar Thailand: Commercial Bankers, Industrial Elite, and Agribusiness Groups." In McVey, Ruth T., ed. 1992. *Southeast Asian Capitalists.* Ithaca, NY: Cornell University Southeast Asia Program.

Sulistyo, Hermawan. 1997. "The Forgotten Years: The Missing History of Indonesia's Mass Slaughter (Jombang-Kediri, 1965–1966)." Ph.D. dissertation, Arizona State University.

The Sun (Kuala Lumpur, Malaysia). 2005. "Campaign against Moral Policing." March 23.

Sunyoto, Agus. 1996. *Banser Berjihad Menumpas PKI.* Tulungagung: Thorqoh Agung.

Surabaya Post. 1991a. "Penerapan Jilbab Tunggu SK Dirjen." February 18.

———. 1991b. "Aini, Arti, Nurul, dan Widy: Bersyukur Meski Harus Tergusur." February 24.

Suryakusuma, Julia I. 1996. "The State and Sexuality in New Order Indonesia." In Sears, Laurie, ed. 1996. *Fantasizing the Feminine in Indonesia.* Durham, NC: Duke University Press.

Syukur, Abdul. 2003. *Gerakan Usroh di Indonesia: Peristiwa Lampung 1989.* Yogyakarta: Ombak.

Tanter, Richard. 1991. "Intelligence Agencies and Third World Militarization: A Case Study of Indonesia, 1966–1989." Ph.D. dissertation, Monash University.

Tapol. 1987. *Indonesia: Muslims on Trial.* London: Tapol.

Tempo (Jakarta). 2001a. "Cerita dari Mosaik Bom Natal." February 25.

———. 2001b. "Nur Dituding, Hidayat Mengelak." February 25.

———. 2001c. "Bom di Jalur Kontak GAM-TNI." February 25.

———. 2001d. "Tamu Misterius Biara Fransiskan." February 25.

———. 2001e. "'Nyanyian' Pengebom Medan." February 25.

———. 2001f. "Kol. Inf. Dasiri Musnar: 'Buktikan Saya Terlibat'." February 25.

———. 2002a. "Telepon Sjafrie di Saku Sang 'Cuak'."January 5.

———. 2002b. "Al-Qaidah 'made in Madiun'?" February 3.

———. 2002c. "Tim Jibril, Al-Qaidah Dari Solo?" February 24.

———. 2002d. "Setelah Intel Melayu Bersatu." February 24.

———. 2002e. "Sapu Bersih Gaya Dr. M." February 24.

———. 2005a. "Uang Palsu Dari Madiun 34." January 30.

———. 2005b. "Persenan buat Agen Pejaten." February 20.

———. 2005c. "Partai Dakwah di Simpang Jalan." August 7.

———. 2005d. "Sebatang Salib yang Dikunci." September 5.

———. 2005e. "Menakar Citra, Mendukung SBY." November 27.

———. 2006a. "Undang-Undang Dengan Definisi Kabur." February 12.

———. 2006b. "Goyangan Tak Kunjung Reda." May 14.

———. 2006c. "Jika Malam Selalu Mencemaskan." May 14.

———. 2006d. "Syariat Islam di Jalur Lambat." May 14.

———. 2006e. "Akibat Menyontek Tetangga."May 14.

———. 2006f. "Pecut Bambu Dari Bulukumba." May 14.

———. 2006g. "Berputar Menuju Sang Kekasih." May 28.

———. 2006h. "Laskar-Laskar Dalam Sorotan." June 25.

———. 2006i. "Wawancara: Yang Tidak Suka Syariat Berlindung di Balik Pancasila." June 25.

———. 2006j. "Soal Lama, Ketegangan Baru." August 20.

———. 2006k. "Setelah Cambukan 40 Kali." August 20.

———. 2006m. "Ketika Batas Religi Meleleh." August 20.

———. 2006n. "Azan Magrib di Bali." August 20.

———. 2006p. "Hidup Rukun di Lembah Dumoga." August 20.

———. 2006q. "Kepahitan Pengikut Sanghyang Kersa." August 20.

———. 2006r. "Setelah Cap Pembangkang Dilekatkan." August 20.

———. 2006s. "Beribu Jalan Menyenangkan Tuhan Dan Umat." November 5.

Tempo Interaktif. 2001. "Wawancara Paul Wolfowitz: 'Aksi Teror di Indonesia Disusupi Al-Qaidah'." November 19.

———. 2004. "Hidayat: PKS Tidak Akan Masuk Kabinet." April 26.

———. 2005. "PKS dan PAN dukung Boediono Masuk Kabinet." December 2.

Torres, Jose Jr. 2001. *Into the Mountains: Hostaged by the Abu Sayyaf*. Quezon City: Claretian Publications.

Tripp, Charles. 2006. *Islam and the Moral Economy: The Challenge of Capitalism.* Cambridge: Cambridge University Press.

Turner, Mark. 1995, "Terrorism and Secession in the Southern Philippines: The Rise of the Abu Sayyaf." *Contemporary Southeast Asia* 17(1): 1–19.

———. 2003. "The Management of Violence in a Conflict Organization: The Case of the Abu Sayyaf." *Public Organization Review* 3(4): 387–401.

Van Bruinessen, Martin. 2003. "Genealogies of Islamic Radicalism in Post-Suharto Indonesia." *South East Asia Research* 10(2): 117–54.

Van Dijk, Kees. 1981. *Rebellion Under the Banner of Islam: The Darul Islam in Indonesia.* The Hague: Martinus Nijhoff.

———. 2001. *A Country in Despair: Indonesia between 1997 and 2000.* Leiden: KITLV Press.

Van Doorn-Harder, Pieternella. 2003. *Women Shaping Islam: Reading the Qur'an in Indonesia.* Urbana: University of Illinois Press.

Vitug, Marites Danguilan, and Glenda Gloria. 2000. *Under The Crescent Moon: Rebellion in Mindanao.* Quezon City: Ateneo Center for Social Policy and Public Affairs.

Wajah Dewan Perwakilan Rakyat Republik Indonesia Pemilihan Umum 1999. 2000. Jakarta: Kompas.

Warren, James Francis. 1985. *The Sulu Zone 1768–1898: The Dynamics of External Trade, Slavery, and Ethnicity in the Transformation of a Southeast Asian Maritime State.* Quezon City: Ateneo de Manila University Press.

Wieviorka, Michele. 2004. *The Making of Terrorism.* Chicago: University of Chicago Press.

Wiktorowicz, Quintan. 2001. *The Management of Islamic Activism: Salafis, the Muslim Brotherhood, and State Power in Jordan.* Albany: SUNY Press.

Winichakul, Thongchai. 1994. *Siam Mapped: A History of the Geo-Body of Siam.* Honolulu: University of Hawai'i Press.

Wolf, Diane L. 2005. *Factory Daughters: Gender, Household Dynamics, and Rural Industrialization on Java.* Berkeley: University of California Press.

List of Reviewers 2006–07

The East-West Center Washington would like to acknowledge the following, who have offered reviews of manuscripts for *Policy Studies*.

Itty Abraham
East-West Center Washington

Jaya Raj Acharya
United States Institute of Peace

Vinod K. Aggarwal
University of California, Berkeley

Muthiah Alagappa
East-West Center Washington

Edward Aspinall
Australian National University

Marc Askew
Victoria University, Melbourne

Dipankar Banerjee
Institute of Peace and Conflict Studies, New Delhi

Sanjay Barbora
Panos South Asia, Guwahati

Upendra Baxi
University of Warwick

Apurba K. Baruah
North Eastern Hill University, Shillong

Sanjib Baruah
Bard College

Thomas Berger
Boston University

Ikrar Nusa Bhakti
Indonesian Institute of Sciences (LIPI), Jakarta

C. Raja Mohan
Nanyang Technological University

Mary P. Callahan
University of Washington

Richard Chauvel
Victoria University, Melbourne

T.J. Cheng
The College of William and Mary

Chu Yun-han
Academia Sinica

Ralph A. Cossa
Pacific Forum CSIS, Honolulu

Neil DeVotta
Hartwick College

Dieter Ernst
East-West Center

Greg Fealy
Australian National University

David Finkelstein
The CNA Corporation

Michael Foley
The Catholic University of America

Sumit Ganguly
Indiana University, Bloomington

Brigham Golden
Columbia University

Michael J. Green
Center for Strategic and International Studies
Georgetown University

Stephan Haggard
University of California, San Diego

Natasha Hamilton
National University of Singapore

Farzana Haniffa
University of Colombo

Rana Hasan
Asian Development Bank

M. Sajjad Hassan
London School of Economics

Eric Heginbotham
RAND Corporation

Donald Horowitz
Duke University

Chinnaiah Jangam
Wagner College

S. Kalyanaraman
Institute for Defence Studies and Analyses, New Delhi

Bengt Karlsson
Uppsala University

Damien Kingsbury
Deakin University

Mahendra Lawoti
Western Michigan University

R. William Liddle
The Ohio State University

Satu P. Limaye
Institute for Defense Analyses

Joseph Chinyong Liow
Nanyang Technological University

Owen M. Lynch
New York University

Gurpreet Mahajan
Jawaharlal Nehru University

Onkar S. Marwah
Independent Consultant, Geneva

Bruce Matthews
Acadia University

Duncan McCargo
University of Leeds

Donald McFetridge
Former U.S. Defense Attaché, Jakarta

Udayon Misra
Dibrugarh University

Pratyoush Onta
Martin Chautari

Andrew Oros
Washington College

Morten Pedersen
United Nations University, Tokyo

Steven Rood
The Asia Foundation, Philippines

Danilyn Rutherford
University of Chicago

Kanchana N. Ruwanpura
University of Southampton

James Scott
Yale University

Amita Shastri
San Francisco State University

Emile C.J. Sheng
Soochow University

John Sidel
London School of Economics

Martin Smith
Independent Analyst, London

Selma Sonntag
Humboldt State University

Ashley South
Independent Consultant

Robert H. Taylor
University of London

Tin Maung Maung Than
Institute of Southeast Asian Studies, Singapore

Willem van Schendel
Amsterdam School for Social science Research

Jayadeva Uyangoda
University of Colombo

Meredith Weiss
East-West Center Washington

Thongchai Winichakul
University of Wisconsin, Madison

Wu Xinbo
Fudan University

Harn Yawnghe
Euro-Burma Office, Brussels

Policy Studies
Previous Publications

(continued next page)

These issues of *Policy Studies* are presently available in print and PDF.
Hardcopies are available through Amazon.com. In Asia, hardcopies of all titles, and electronic
copies of Southeast Asia titles are available through the Institute of Southeast Asian Studies,
Singapore at 30 Heng Mui Keng Terrace, Pasir Panjang Road, Singapore 119614. Website:
http://bookshop.iseas.edu.sg/

Online at: www.eastwestcenterwashington.org/publications

Policy Studies
Previous Publications continued

(continued next page)

These issues of *Policy Studies* are presently available in print and PDF.
Hardcopies are available through Amazon.com. In Asia, hardcopies of all titles, and electronic
copies of Southeast Asia titles are available through the Institute of Southeast Asian Studies,
Singapore at 30 Heng Mui Keng Terrace, Pasir Panjang Road, Singapore 119614. Website:
http://bookshop.iseas.edu.sg/
Online at: www.eastwestcenterwashington.org/publications

Policy Studies
Previous Publications continued

Policy Studies 5
The Papua Conflict: Jakarta's Perceptions
and Policies
Richard Chauvel, Victoria University, Melbourne
Ikrar Nusa Bhakti, Indonesian Institute of Sciences,
Jakarta

Policy Studies 4
Beijing's Tibet Policy: Securing Sovereignty
and Legitimacy
Allen Carlson, Cornell University

Policy Studies 3
Security Operations in Aceh: Goals,
Consequences, and Lessons
Rizal Sukma, Centre for Strategic and International
Studies, Jakarta

Policy Studies 2
The Free Aceh Movement (GAM): Anatomy of
a Separatist Organization
Kirsten E. Schulze, London School of Economics

2003
Policy Studies 1
The Aceh Peace Process: Why it Failed
Edward Aspinall, University of Sydney
Harold Crouch, Australian National University

These issues of *Policy Studies* are presently available in print and PDF.
Hardcopies are available through Amazon.com. In Asia, hardcopies of all titles, and electronic
copies of Southeast Asia titles are available through the Institute of Southeast Asian Studies,
Singapore at 30 Heng Mui Keng Terrace, Pasir Panjang Road, Singapore 119614. Website:
http://bookshop.iseas.edu.sg/

Online at: www.eastwestcenterwashington.org/publications

Printed in the United States
136647LV00009B/84/P